A Guide to the Diagnostic Teaching of Arithmetic

Third Edition

Fredricka K. Reisman

University of Georgia

Charles E. Merrill Publishing Company
A Bell & Howell Company
Columbus Toronto London Sydney

Published by
Charles E. Merrill Publishing Company
A Bell & Howell Company
Columbus, Ohio 43216

This book was set in Times Roman and Kabel.
Production Coordination: Judith Rose Sacks

Photo Credits

pp. 3, 87, 129, 137—Strix Pix   p. 21—Phillips Photo Illustrators   pp. 39, 53—Celia
Drake   p. 65—Barbara Lagomarsino   p. 113—© photo by Jean-Claude Lejeune

Library of Congress Catalog Card Number: 81-86091
International Standard Book Number: 0-675-09879-3
Printed in the United States of America
3 4 5 6 7 8 9 10—86 85 84 83 82

FOREWORD

Teaching arithmetic effectively to every child is a goal for every concerned teacher. This book offers a strategy and point of view to help work toward that goal: *diagnostic teaching*. Neither teaching nor learning arithmetic is an easy task; both the teacher and the student have to work. This book recognizes the complexities in the teaching and learning of arithmetic and provides guidelines to facilitate the arithmetic teacher's job. These pages do not contain ready-made solutions to the problems of teaching. Rather, they put forth some processes, in the diagnostic teaching cycle, to assist the concerned and hardworking teacher.

Teaching that is diagnostic in nature attempts to identify the child's level of performance and all the relevant information that contributes to that performance. Then the material to be learned is analyzed into its component parts. Finally, an instructional sequence is implemented for the child that blends the child's cognitive and emotional status with the proper part of the task to be learned. It is important to recognize that these principles of the diagnostic teaching cycle apply to group instruction just as naturally as to individual instruction.

Teaching that is diagnostic in nature attempts to identify the child's level of performance and all the relevant information that contributes to that performance. Then the material to be learned is analyzed into its component parts. Finally, an instructional sequence is implemented for the child that blends the child's cognitively and emotional status with the proper part of the task to be learned. It is important to recognize that these principles of the diagnostic teaching cycle apply to group instruction just as naturally as to individual instruction.

This book is practical in that it illustrates, by principles and by examples, the *process* of diagnostic teaching of arithmetic. It is a definitive source on the purposes, nature, and use of diagnostic teaching. The diagnostic teaching model provides a framework and guide. Further, the book discusses several tools to assist in diagnostic teaching. This makes the *Guide* a reference that the teacher will want to keep handy and turn to often. Its ultimate practicality is that it can help the teacher do a more effective job in helping each student learn arithmetic.

It is unfortunate if teachers view diagnosis as something to be used only when there is a learning difficulty requiring remediation. To be sure, effective remediation requires diagnosis, and the *Guide* assists teachers with this problem. But Professor Reisman offers a much more positive approach (she uses the word *prevention*): diagnostic teaching can be used to anticipate and avoid learning difficulties. The matching of the current level of performance and the material to be learned is certainly appropriate for instruction with every child, not just those with a learning difficulty.

Surely every teacher recognizes that there is an affective dimension to learning, school, and mathematics, but some may not be sure how to develop positive attitudes in students. The *Guide* provides a cogent introduction to theories of affective behavior, gives advice on assessing how students feel about arithmetic, and discusses ways to develop positive affect.

Professor Reisman presents diagnostic teaching of arithmetic as an understanding of the child, an understanding of the subject matter, and the blending of the two during instruction. The *Guide* provides many suggestions for implementing diagnostic teaching strategies, and its use will make mathematics teaching more successful and enjoyable.

James W. Wilson

Head, Department of Mathematics Education
University of Georgia

PREFACE

This book describes a preventative model of diagnosis in arithmetic of interest to preservice, inservice, general classroom, and special education teachers. Both the problems students have in learning mathematics and suggestions for remediation of these problems are presented. Task analyses of time telling, counting, and addition of fractions are presented to encourage teachers to think about goals and sequencing these goals in planning instruction. Also, diagnostic tasks are described that utilize concrete materials and pictures as well as abstract symbols.

This book is not a methods book; rather, it is a supplement to methods and content books in mathematics. The emphasis is on a diagnostic teaching model that is sequential and cyclical in nature. The author's philosophy is that understanding the psychological nature of the mathematics curriculum and its implications for teaching can aid in the prevention as well as remediation of mathematics difficulties.

A brief comparison is made between norm- and criterion-referenced tests. A mathematics inventory is developed to serve as a model for teacher-made tests. Examples of common errrors students make in mathematics are presented as well as models for graphing individual and class profiles for summarizing students' strengths and weaknesses. However, the emphasis is not on error analysis but rather on using the errors in relationship to concerns such as those listed in the book under "possible causes of difficulties."

Psychological hierarchies and taxonomies are applied to mathematics topics. For example, some of Piaget's tasks on conservation and seriation, based upon developmental psychology, serve as diagnostic activities. Brownell's and

Gagne's taxonomies that describe the psychological nature of mathematics curriculum are translated into diagnostic mathematics tasks. Bloom's taxonomy is presented as an aid in developing test items at higher levels of cognition as well as the more usual "recognize" or "recall" types. And Bruner's distinction of representing a learning task at the enactive, iconic, and symbolic levels is included.

Diagnosing in the affective domain is emphasized. Included are Maslow's hierarchy of needs, Krathwohl's affective domain taxonomy, Carl Rogers' comparison of psychotherapy to the student–teacher relationship, and Osgood's semantic differential technique to assess attitudes. A brief summary of literature on math anxiety is presented, and the process of cognitive monitoring —thinking about one's thinking—is offered as one way of dealing with feelings of anxiety about mathematics.

I wish to thank William Hays, University of Texas at Austin, for his support of the importance of meshing mathematics with psychology. To E. Paul Torrance, University of Georgia, my gratitude for his continuing encouragement and guidance. To Kathryn Blake, University of Georgia, appreciation for recognition of the diagnostic teaching system that is the underlying structure of this book. To colleagues at the University of Georgia—especially those in the Division of Elementary Education, in mathematics education, and in special education—thank you for your support in helping me refine my thoughts regarding diagnostic teaching of mathematics. To my secretary, Pat Greene, my thanks for helping with typing the manuscript.

I am grateful to the staff at Charles E. Merrill, especially Julie Estadt, Judy Sacks, and Lynn Walcoff.

Finally, to my students—you who guide children in learning mathematics —thank you for replacing anxiety and gaps in learning with enjoyment and diagnostic teaching of mathematics.

Fredricka K. Reisman

Professor and Chair,
Division of Elementary Education
University of Georgia

CONTENTS

To my father, my daughter, my son-in-law, and to the memory of my mother

PART 1

A DIAGNOSTIC TEACHING MODEL

Part One of this book describes a model for teaching elementary school mathematics that is preventive as well as remedial in nature. Instead of focusing on teaching to weaknesses, teachers are encouraged to help students *avoid* learning problems in mathematics. Typical causes of difficulties in mathematics are discussed, including the following:

1. Gaps in mathematical foundation
2. Lack of readiness
3. Emotional problems
4. Deprived environment
5. Poor teaching
6. Learning disabilities

The Diagnostic Teaching Cycle is a model that directs the teacher to assess the strengths and weaknesses of an individual student or of an entire class in mathematics performance. As the steps in the model are followed, ongoing or formative evaluation occurs. This formative evaluation provides corrective feedback so that a minimum amount of time goes by before trouble spots are noticed. Consequently, several causes of trouble, such as conceptual gaps, anxiety that is inhibiting, instruction that is too abstract, and/or presentation of curriculum that is beyond a student's cognitive level can be prevented.

1

At the end of the first chapter there is a discussion of issues that concern teachers of the eighties. Also presented is a comparison of the Diagnostic Teaching Cycle to creative problem solving and to developing an individual educational plan.

Finally, in Part One the reader is introduced to the technique of *task analysis*. Throughout the book, the reader is encouraged to use task analysis to prevent gaps in the learning hierarchy. The goals of a task that has been analyzed can then be sequenced to facilitate learning. The task analysis of time telling is an example of how a task analysis can make apparent an instructional sequence that has been followed for years but that does not enhance learning.

1

Introduction to Diagnostic Teaching of Arithmetic

The approach to teaching presented in this book is based on an educational focus rather than on a medical model of "diagnose, prescribe, remediate." The goal of diagnostic teaching that underlies this approach is to *prevent* learning problems whenever possible. In order to prevent unncecessary difficulties the teacher must be aware of the intricacies involved in teaching arithmetic. Major concerns that a teacher should keep in mind include the following:

1. Do I as a teacher understand the mathematics that I am attempting to teach?
2. Have I selected mathematics that is appropriate and relevant to the basic mathematics learning needs and abilities of my students?
3. Have I selected topics to be taught in a sequence that enhances learning or do I follow the basal text page by page without regard for individual learning differences?
4. Have I assessed whether or not students know how to do requisite tasks that underlie the mathematics goal I am introducing?
5. Have I provided enough activities at the concrete level so that students have a foundation for constructing abstract ideas, or do I only assign paper and pencil tasks? (This also applies to the middle grades as well as secondary and higher educational levels.)
6. Do I provide sufficient and appropriate practice activities after I introduce a new topic? Do I build reviews into my instructional sequence?
7. Do I consider the emotional aspects of learning mathematics as I plan for instruction? Am I aware of students who display "math anxiety," who are overtly resistant to or rebellious toward learning arithmetic, who cheat on mathematics exams? How do I feel when I have to teach mathematics?

Diagnostic Teaching Described

Diagnostic teaching, which involves guiding a child to learn a portion of curriculum, is a two-part approach. First, the developmental level at which a child is performing cognitively must be identified. Second, the task to be learned must be analyzed in order to determine how many components of the task the child has already acquired. In elementary school mathematics this second phase of diagnostic approach, analyzing the mathematical relationships, is the crux of diagnostic teaching. When the teacher is aware of the relationships that are basic to mathematical concepts and generalizations, he or she is better able to make decisions regarding selection of curriculum and use of effective instructional techniques that are most appropriate to the learner.

For example, in order for a child to compute a long division problem, he or she must be able to multiply and subtract. To multiply, he or she must translate the idea of a certain number of groups, each of a particular size, into a multiplication example (five groups of three$\Rightarrow$five threes$\Rightarrow$5 × 3). In order to subtract, the child must find the remainder when given a whole and a known part, and if renaming (borrowing) is involved, have a working knowledge of how a place value system operates.

Unless the teacher can analyze the relation or task to be learned into its requisite parts, he or she will not understand the child's learning problems. The meshing of the components of the curriculum with the cognitive level at which the child is performing is the heart of diagnostic teaching.

Of course, diagnostic teaching is not only for children having difficulty in arithmetic. All children—whether they are slow learners, average, or very bright—profit from diagnostic teaching because of its basic assumption, the necessity for meshing curriculum with the student's learning characteristics.

New sequences of instruction also may emerge from diagnostic teaching. For example, consider teaching the skill of telling time to the precision of a minute. The traditional approach has been to teach time on the hour first, then to the half-hour, and next to five minutes after the hour. Children have not been taught time to the minute until the last step in the instructional sequence. In fact, many elementary school mathematics texts introduce the fractional idea of "half after" and "a quarter after" the hour prior to the concept of "so many minutes after." However, when looking at how children learn to count, we see that they learn to count by *ones* first. Yet, they are not exposed to telling time to the minute, which is based on counting by ones, until the latter part of the time-telling sequence—a goal that usually is introduced during second or third grade. This seems in opposition to the natural development of counting. Also, children may become fixated on the positions of time to the hour and to the half hour, thus making it more difficult for them to learn to tell time to the minute. When we analyze the task from a mathematical view and mesh our findings with our knowledge of how children first learn to count, we discover that our sequence of instruction has been backward.

Further investigation, making use of the concrete mode of learning, has indicated that children can reproduce time on a clock face before they can identify it. Thus, setting time on a clock face should precede reading time on a clock face. This sequence usually is ignored and, in fact, time-telling instruction often starts at the iconic, or picture, level (Bruner, 1963). Bruner has labeled three levels of representing information about the real world as "enactive," "iconic," and "symbolic." The enactive level is the first representation a child uses. It involves active involvement of the child and may be translated into an educational meaning by the child's manipulation of concrete objects to learn about their shape and size or the number of objects in a set. The next level of representation of reality, the iconic level, deals with images and is exemplified educationally by the use of pictures of sets of objects. The highest level is the symbolic level and involves words and numerals (e.g., use of the numeral *5* or the spoken or written word *five* to represent the number fiveness is symbolic). Thus, the use of mathematics workbooks in kindergarten and the early grades involves the iconic and symbolic levels and should follow object manipulation, which is the enactive level. These may be thought of as levels of representing curriculum or content to be learned.

Since most young children are used to working with the idea of a number line, time-telling instruction can begin with the child's counting from 0 to 60 on a number line. The concept of one-to-one correspondence as the child matches each number with a minute mark can be demonstrated.

A clock face has been developed in research on time-telling instruction (Reisman, 1968) that is based on this notion of reinforcing the "counting by ones" concept. After giving a child experiences in counting from 1 to 60 on a

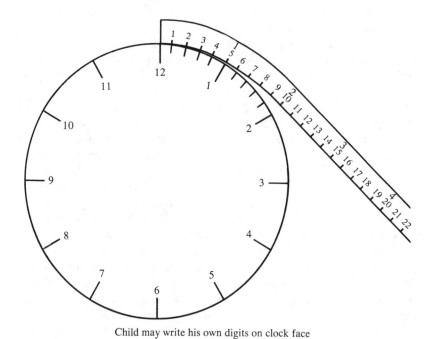

Child may write his own digits on clock face

FIGURE 1   Reisman Experimental Clock Face

plastic, snap-on number line, the child then was guided to generalize from this snap-on number line to the 60-minute marks on a clock face. The snap-on number line (from 1 to 60) matched up with the 60-minute marks on the clock face.

The snap-on number line also had a number line with 0 to 12 written on it. The numeral 1 on the 12-item number line corresponded to the numeral 5 on the 60-item number line; the numeral 2 on the 12-item number line corresponded to the numeral 10 on the 60-item number line; the numeral 3 corresponded to the numeral 15; etc. The 12-item number line also corresponded to the clock-face digits illustrating the underlying multiplication relationships that one group of five is 5, two groups of five are 10, three groups of five are 15, . . . eleven groups of five are 55, and twelve groups of five are 60. Thus, the digit 2 on a clock face means two groups of 5 minutes after the hour or 10 minutes after the hour, while the digit 11 means eleven groups of 5 or 55 minutes after the hour. The children described the digit 12 on the clock face as showing twelve fives or 60 minutes after the hour and said that this was another name for zero minutes after the next hour.

Since the children were actively involved in manipulating the snap-on number line, in naming the minute marks from 1 through 60, and in matching the digits on the clock face with multiples of 5 on the snap-on number line, they were able to analyze a clock face and describe the function of each part.

The minute hand alone was then attached and used as a counter for the snap-on, (now circular) 60-item number line. Then the hour hand was attached and used as an indicator of how many times the minute hand had traversed the entire clock face.

Children as young as first graders and a few in kindergarten learned to write the numerals from 1 to 12, properly sequenced, on the Plexiglas clock face as they used the snap-on number line.

The language in the initial stages of instruction consisted of "so many minutes after the hour." In my experience in teaching children to tell time, I have found that an early changeover to the language "before the hour" is confusing to the child. In describing his investigations on learning time concepts, Piaget (1955, 1966) offered an explanation for this before-after confusion.

The time-telling example just discussed illustrates how teachers can improve instruction when they become aware of relations among task components and learner characteristics. (See pp. 31–32, 33–36 in regard to time-telling task analysis.)

Diagnostic teaching, then, is a process of determining facts that need to be taken into account in making instructional decisions. Curriculum decisions are dependent upon diagnosing the needs of a particular society, of a unique population within that society, or of an individual. Decisions about what methods of instruction are most appropriate for teaching a particular topic to a particular type of learner also are determined by diagnosis. Diagnosis involves looking at both the curriculum to be taught and the method of instruction. It may involve asking the following questions: Is the curriculum that I am attempting to teach this child appropriate to his or her needs, both present and future? Is the concept to be taught appropriate to his or her level of cognitive functioning? Is a learning discrepancy or disability preventing the child from learning? Has the child acquired the necessary prerequisites in order to learn this curriculum? What is the most appropriate method of instruction that I can use for the learner to facilitate acquisition of this knowledge? Why has this student not acquired this portion of curriculum, or why is he or she not able to perform this task?

The elementary school teacher needs to consider the appropriateness of the mathematics curriculum as related to the intellectual, social, emotional, and psychological needs of the student, and the suitability of past methods of instruction both to the curriculum taught and to the manner in which the student learns. A comparison of a student's performance in learning mathematics with performance in learning other disciplines can be helpful. The teacher should also review and analyze scores on achievement and diagnostic tests, as well as results of teacher-built instruments used to identify difficulties with mathematics,

Possible Causes of Difficulties

Why do some children have difficulty learning arithmetic? Problems with mathematics performance may emerge from many sources. Difficulties in learning arithmetic may stem from gaps in a child's mathematical foundation, lack of readiness, emotional problems, deprived environment, poor teaching, or from a variety of learning disabilities.

Gaps in Mathematical Foundation

For a child to be able to display skill in arithmetic computation, he or she must have a basic understanding of the mathematical relationships underlying the computation. If there is a gap in the conceptual foundation of mathematics, the student will not be able to perform mathematical tasks that are dependent upon this foundation. For example, place value is based upon an awareness of multiplication ideas, division is related to both multiplication and subtraction, and addition of fractions with unlike denominators is based upon using the multiplicative identity to find equivalent fractions.

In looking at the mathematics curriculum, one must consider the *level* of difficulty involved. If the curriculum contains an abundance of material that is too advanced or too difficult, a student may become frustrated and give up.

On the other hand, a curriculum that is too easy leads to boredom, and more talented students may also give up. Does the curriculum offer motivation to the student? Can the teacher take advantage of student interest to "hook" the student on learning mathematics or must he or she follow a school policy that says, "Be on page 234 on December 5 or you won't finish the book, and you must finish the book"? In other words, is the book being taught instead of the child?

Is the mathematics implicit in a situation of interest to the child? A study by Braun (1969) found that low achievers comprehended to an appreciable degree that work with fractions was related to percentages when a homemade radio was used as the visual aid. The children made workable dials using a cycle range for AM of 550–1600 kilocycles and for FM of 80–108 megacycles. The students noted distance in numbers between various stations on a dial beginning with zero, then translated these distances into fractional parts of the dial and, finally, proceeded to rename the fractions into percentages. Braun concluded that the students were dealing with a matter in which they had daily interest because most of them had radios in their homes.

Another concern might be that the student has changed schools and undergone an accompanying change in the mathematics program. With an emphasis on a "back to basics" curriculum, change may result in a new focus on computation using the basic operations of addition, subtraction, multiplication, and division. Relations underlying the various computational algorithms must be understood in order to avoid creating gaps in one's mathematical foundation.

In order to visualize effects of a gap in the child's mathematics foundation, think of a weak or broken rung on a ladder. Such a rung can either prevent you from climbing any further, or if you skip over the broken rung, can make you feel uneasy because you know it's there. The rungs on a ladder are the necessary prerequisites for reaching the top.

For a child to perform a simple operation on numbers, he or she must have the necessary prerequisites needed to reach the top of the ladder. For example, in order to understand the algorithm $\begin{array}{r} 23 \\ -9 \end{array}$ the child must know these prerequisites:

—that 23 means two tens and three ones;
—that 9 means nine ones;
—that two tens and three ones may be renamed as one ten and thirteen ones;
—that by renaming two tens and three ones as one ten and thirteen ones, we change only the name but not the number;
—that we obtain this new name by using place value: for every group of ten ones, we must rename them as one ten in order to record the number, since after nine ones, we have no single digit to record ten

ones; so we exchange ten ones for one ten, thus moving over to the tens place. In subtraction, when more ones are needed, we merely undo this action, and change one of the tens back to ten ones. These ten ones are added to the ones already there;

—that since the number to be subtracted may not exceed nine ones (or it would have already been renamed as one ten and so many ones), it is sufficient to rename only one of the tens as ten ones, to be added to the number of ones already present;

—that 13 minus 9 equals 4;

—that one ten minus zero tens is one ten;

—" − " means "subtract";

—that the top numeral in a subtraction example stands for the whole;

—that the bottom one stands for the known part that is to be subtracted to find the unknown part:

$$\begin{array}{r} \text{Whole} \\ -\,\text{Known Part} \\ \hline \text{Unknown Part} \end{array}$$

If any one of these concepts is unknown to the child, he or she may have difficulty with this subtraction algorithm. This is why you will see $\begin{array}{r} 23 \\ -\,9 \\ \hline 26 \end{array}$. The child is making the problem fit what he or she can handle. The child does not know how to get enough ones to subtract nine ones; so he or she breaks a ground rule and subtracts some of the whole from the part.

It would be wise to provide the child with experiences in place value and then to diagnose if the weakness is here. The child may be able to regroup ten tongue depressors as one bundle of ten at the concrete manipulative level, but he or she may not see a connection to recording numbers as:

1
2
3
.
.
.
7
8
9
10
11
12

.
.
.
19
20

A place value chart will help.

tens	ones
	1
	2
	.
	.
	.
	8
	9 Renaming occurs here
1	0
1	1
1	2
.	.
1	9
2	0

You must determine if the gap is at the symbolic or concrete level. Since the pictorial level lies between the concrete and symbolic levels of representing numbers, you might guide the child to portray the example $\frac{23}{-9}$ as shown in Figure 2.

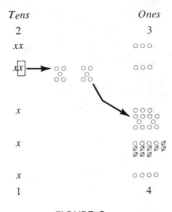

FIGURE 2

As the teacher you must know what prerequisite concepts are necessary for subtracting a number represented by one digit from a number represented by two digits when renaming is necessary. Then, after you find out what the student knows and does not know, you can select appropriate materials and methods and proceed to fill in gaps in the child's mathematical foundations.

Lack of Readiness

Give a five-year-old a basket of seven apples to count. If she counts in either of the two ways shown in Figure 3, she has not mastered one-to-one correspondence, which is basic to any work with numbers.

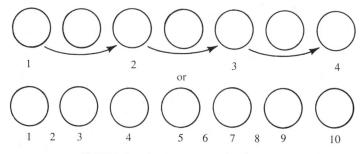

FIGURE 3 Example of Rote Counting

If she cannot select more or fewer objects, she lacks a necessary prerequisite for number work. If she cannot label a group of objects with its appropriate number name or numeral, she is not yet ready for computation. The child may not be able to reproduce a set having the same number of objects as a model set. She may not be able to put groups with different numbers of objects in order by going from smallest to largest. She may not recognize that two sets having the same number property (each having the same number of objects) continue to have the same number property even when one set is spread out so that it takes up more space than the other. And she will not understand our place value system of numeration unless she has the concept of many-to-one, the idea that a numeral placed in the tens place means so many tens rather than so many ones. This is a multiplicative idea; yet the curriculum includes place value in first grade and multiplication principles in third grade.

Emotional Problems

Failure in arithmetic can be caused by emotional problems, but it also can cause emotional problems.* Some children already have developed a fear of arithmetic before they come to school. They may have heard a parent talk

---

*See also the discussion regarding math anxiety, pp. 125–126.

about difficulty or failure in arithmetic and subconsciously may identify with this parent. A child's previous teacher may have been threatened by the prospect of teaching arithmetic and conveyed these insecurities to the child. Perhaps the child has had a personal experience with mathematics that was negative or unpleasant. She or he may have been shortchanged at the store and received a severe rebuff from a parent who accused the child of being stupid or of not knowing how to count.

Sometimes a parent's occupation is mathematically oriented. Children of these parents may have difficulty in arithmetic either because they would rather fail than compete with their parent or because they try so hard to succeed that they block their learning.

Unfortunately, some parents make their children buy parental love with high grades. Since mathematics is a high-status subject, a child in this position consciously or subconsciously may do poorly or even fail in order to maintain his or her autonomy. In effect, this child is saying, "Won't you love me for me and not for the high grades?"

I have tested several children having difficulty with mathematics and some with reading problems who seemed to fall into an emotionally based pattern. These children scored in the 115 to 140+ range on the Wechsler Intelligence Scale for Children–Revised (WISC–R); yet they were at least two years below grade level in one or both of these academic areas on standardized achievement tests. The pattern that appeared throughout involved the parents of these children. In the majority of cases, the parents were achievement-oriented and were quick to announce that they expected their children to maintain a high level of performance. In those cases where the parents had been informed of the child's IQ score by the school or by a psychologist, they were even more upset that their child, with this high ability level, was not working to capacity. The psychologist had interpreted the findings in many of these cases as the child's refusal to buy parental love with high grades. This usually was described as a subconscious act on the child's part because he or she was unaware of the reasons for the low scores. Similarly, the parents were not aware that this was the demand that they were projecting to their child. The merit of such an interpretation is uncertain and should probably be categorized as a hypothesis, but it is a hypothesis worth considering. At any rate, the results of pointing out this possibility to both the child and the parents where treatment involved a psychologist working with the family were successful in some cases. Arithmetic and reading, the two high-status school subjects, seemed to be the areas most affected under this hypothesis. Indeed, if a child perceived his or her parents as demanding that their love be bought with high grades and he or she was unwilling to do this—either consciously or subconsciously—what better areas than mathematics and reading could there be in which to fail?

The following studies have investigated parental effect on children's achievement in school. Mumpower and Riggs (1970) have hypothesized that there is a positive relationship between a child's achievement in word accuracy and the parental use of pressure on the child for educational achievement. They have suggested that knowledge of this relationship might be helpful to the teacher of reading since it may explain why some children do so well in word accuracy while doing poorly in comprehension. Two groups were matched on age, sex, grade, IQ, and mental age; any problems that could have arisen because of differences in race were "controlled by using only white children." One group showed overachievement in word accuracy by one full grade and their comprehension was normal. The other group showed no overachievement in either word accuracy or comprehension. To find factors that might account for the first group's overachievement in word accuracy, a study of the material contained in the individuals' folders was made and 10 factors were found. Since the hypothesis was that individuals in Group 1 would show more of these factors than would those in Group 2, it was necessary to test only the significant differences in the factors of Group 1 and Group 2 that were in the yes-no or no-yes cells. The most significant difference between Groups 1 and 2 was that the parents exerted pressure on the children in Group 1 for good grades. These findings suggest that children who overachieved in word accuracy exhibited certain characteristics that children who achieved normally did not exhibit. The overachievers expended much effort in school, evidently in response to pressure exerted on them by their parents. There was a tendency for the overachievers to show signs of emotional disturbance as related to school and for their parents to fail to either understand or accept their limitations. The authors concluded that the children who overachieved in word accuracy were subjected to more pressure than was necessarily good for them. They succeeded by achieving on a lower level of learning, which involved rote learning, but failed to do well in comprehension, which required a higher level of mental maturity. The parents of the overachievers needed to understand their children better and to accept their limitations.

Pierce (1961) has suggested that male underachievers have particularly poor relationships with their fathers. McGillivray (1964) has described the underachiever's home environment as being more punitive. Rouman (1956) found that among 400 children referred to a Los Angeles guidance clinic, academic failure was greatest among those having no adult male in the home. Elementary-school-age children were more dependent upon the father's guidance than were younger children. Greatest withdrawal was shown by those having a mother who was working outside the home, and the age of the child was a big factor in determining the child's major problems. The working mothers contributed to 25 percent of the total number of cases in need of psychological help, and girls made up a fourth of the cases sent for guidance. Fraiberg (1977) advocates that mothers are their children's best caretakers. However, Kagan, Kearsley, and Zelazo (1978) refute this position and bring into question reported negative effects of day care on later adjustment. In regard to sex-related issues, Kessler and McKenna (1978) provide a constructivist view of the development of gender concepts that emphasizes social influences rather than biological characteristics.

An open and investigative approach is a necessary part of a diagnostic strategy if we are to identify the real problem. It may be that the initial identification is in the area of mathematics, but a comparison of a student's overall performance as well as a history of her or his performance in mathematics often leads to a further look at parent-child relations or parent-teacher-child interactions.

Since arithmetic is a high-status subject, failures in arithmetic achievement can cause emotional problems. Some of these actually take a physical form, and a child may break out in a cold sweat or become nauseated at the onset of mathematical activities. A few failures in arithmetic can snowball quickly and cause a child to lose confidence in her or his academic ability in general.

Deprived Environment

All children are exposed to quantitative experiences in their environment at a very early age. When one recognizes that his or her friend has more candy, skips rope for a longer time, runs a greater distance in a given time, or gets the round cookie instead of the square one, the child is dealing with mathematics. However, children who are disadvantaged have meager experiences in number situations. In their book *Teaching Strategies for the Culturally Disadvantaged,* Taba and Elkins (1966) have described the effects of a deprived environment on learning mathematics concepts:

> Research indicates that the condition of life in slums tends to be meagre in all respects. Slum life provides a minimum range of stimulation and minimum opportunity to manipulate objects or to experiment with them in an orderly manner. Monotony of input limits expressiveness of the output and the ability to perceive precise relationships or other abstract qualities, such as size, shape distance, and time. (p. 7)*

The teacher, therefore, must provide the following basic quantitative experiences for disadvantaged children: manipulating objects to form groups having different number properties; matching objects in a one-to-one correspon-

---

*From *Teaching Strategies for the Culturally Disadvantaged* by Hilda Taba and Deborah Elkins (Chicago: Rand McNally, 1966, p. 7). Reprinted by permission.

dence; guiding children to abstract concepts of size, shape, or number from groups of objects; moving from manipulation of objects to activities with pictures of the objects; and, finally, guiding children to work with symbols that stand for the number of objects in a group.

Poor Teaching

Unfortunately, all of the reasons for children's learning difficulties in mathematics do not reside in the child or society. Some problems stem from the school setting itself, more specifically, weaknesses of the teacher.

Concrete manipulatory experiences must be provided in sufficient amounts for each child to build a foundation of such basic mathematical relationships as one-to-one and many-to-one correspondence; more than and less than; combining objects as a model for addition; separating groups as a model for subtraction; and naming the number property, the "how muchness" of a group with word names (e.g., *five*) and with numerals (e.g., *5*). Unless opportunities for learning these basic relationships have been provided, the teacher has been delinquent.

Sometimes the teacher creates an atmosphere in the mathematics classroom that does not encourage questioning when an idea is not understood. Often a child will assume that a hazy idea will clear up as time goes on but instead finds that a gap in his or her foundation has emerged. Teachers must diagnose constantly to pick up these gaps. Informal paper-pencil quizzes where grades are not recorded and talking with the child can help to identify the child's trouble without being a threat. An analysis as to whether the child is experiencing difficulty in mathematics as a result of a weak conceptual structure or because of a lack of consolidation of facts necessary to build the particular concepts is essential. Brownell and Hendrickson (1950) have explained that *facts* are arbitrary associations and contain a minimum amount of meaning. They are learned in a rather rote manner, and, thus, are in need of practice exercises until they can be handled with facility. Concepts, however, are a different matter. The learning of concepts depends upon conditions associated with the learner, the nature of the task, and the abstracting process.

Learning Disabilities

Inefficient searching strategies, inability to retrieve labels, inability to produce written responses, poor short-term and/or long-term memory, poor spatial relations, impaired communication, distractibility, and excessive fatigability are symptoms of learning disabilities. Suggestions for diagnostic teaching of mathematics to children displaying one or more of these characteristics are included in *Teaching Mathematics to Children with Special Needs* (Reisman & Kauffman, 1980).

Comparison with Other Subjects

When a teacher identifies areas of difficulty in learning mathematics, he or she often compares the student's performance in learning mathematics with performance in learning other disciplines. This affords a baseline of information for the student's academic achievement in general. If overall achievement is low, an investigation of a child's total educational experience is warranted, as is the obtaining of some measures of ability. Is the low achievement in all areas a function of the youngster's out-of-school environment, or is it due to limited ability? Of course, one must realize that low test scores sometimes need to be scrutinized because they may be a reflection of an inappropriate test.

If the area of low achievement is apparent in mathematics alone, then the causes may be emotional in nature or may possibly stem from ineffective mathematics teaching. I tested several children who were failing arithmetic and doing well in other subjects. One girl in seventh grade admitted that she had a man teacher for the first time and was embarrassed to ask questions when she did not understand something in math class. She was usually a good student and believed that "things would clear up" as they went along. However, things did not clear up; in fact, they became progressively worse until the day she came home with a D grade on her report card. This grade prompted a teacher-parent conference; consequently, the girl was referred to a university-based clinic for diagnosis. The results of the diagnosis were discussed with both the parents and the girl's mathematics teacher who encouraged her to speak up when she needed help. The teacher initiated a diagnostic approach in his teaching and told how he now identified other students with learning difficulties and found that these difficulties were remedied easily once they were diagnosed. He said this case had made him aware for the first time that low performance on class tests may stem from a myriad of reasons and that he would question his students about their answers instead of just recording test results.

Another student also was doing well in all areas except arithmetic. This boy was in third grade and his parents were worried that he would not be admitted to engineering school if his grades in math did not drastically improve. The father was an engineer and wanted the boy to follow in his footsteps. An analysis of the boy's mathematical concepts, computation skills, and verbal problem-solving ability showed that he made many errors in computation, although he had a good grasp of concepts and did fairly well in verbal problem solving. It was ascertained that his grades in arithmetic were based mainly on teacher-made tests that were computational in nature and thus reflected only his weakness in mathematics without showing his conceptualization level. It was suggested to the parents that they ease up on a definite career decision for the boy at this time and that instead of emphasizing his one weak area, they start reinforcing his successes. The teacher also built tests that would sample more than just computation skills and mapped out a plan to help the boy improve his computation performance by using practice exercises and praise for his effort.

Diagnostic Teaching—Now and in the Future

Using the diagnostic teaching approach, teachers of the eighties can deal effectively with a number of concerns related to current and future educational needs. Teachers in today's classrooms are undergoing role changes as a result of a variety of circumstances. These changes in expectations of what a classroom teacher should be able to accomplish are related to a variety of issues. These issues concern:

1. low SAT scores
2. results of national assessments (e.g., National Assessment of Educational Progress, NAEP) showing areas in need of improvement—especially consumer skills
3. societal pressures for "back-to-basics"
4. continued funding of programs designated for improvement of mathematics instruction
5. sex differences in achievement in mathematics
6. feminine awareness concerning *math anxiety*
7. federal legislation such as Public Law 94–142

There are conflicting views regarding how to interpret and deal with these issues. There are no ready-made answers; there are no recipes. In some cases teachers are expected to perform instructional tasks for which they have received minimal training—often only one course—as in the case of preparing regular classroom teachers to teach special education students who have been mainstreamed into the regular classroom. Thus, teachers must be creative in their attempt to solve professional problems. Needed are originality and flexibility in thinking, fluency in generating possible solutions to problems, and resistance to premature closure during decision making. These are characteristics of a creative thinker.

Diagnostic Teaching Compared to Creative Problem Solving

Creative problem solving (see also Osborn, 1963; Parnes, 1967; Riley, 1980; Shotick & Reisman, 1979; Torrance, 1979) is closely related to the Diagnostic Teaching Cycle, which is detailed in chapter 2. Keep in mind the steps in diagnostic teaching as described in this book when you consider the steps involved in creative problem solving. The creative problem-solving process is as follows:

1. Become aware that a problem exists and then proceed to identify the *real* problem.
2. List possible and alternative solutions.
3. Evaluate these solutions according to specific criteria.
4. Select one of the solutions and try it.
5. Evaluate the solution's effectiveness in terms of success or lack of success in solving the problem.

Diagnostic Teaching and Individual Educational Plans in Mathematics

The creative problem solving and diagnostic teaching models are useful aids when an individual educational plan in mathematics (IEPM) is developed by an IEP team (see Reisman & Kauffman, 1980) as required by P.L. 94–142.

P.L. 94–142 is federal law mandating that every student be provided a free and appropriate education in the least restrictive environment. This law is often referred to as *mainstreaming*; however, this is a misleading label for P.L. 94–142. Mainstreaming means placing in the regular classroom students who formerly spent their school day in some other educational setting, e.g., a special education class or resource room. According to P.L. 94–142, mainstreaming should occur only if the regular classroom provides the most appropriate least restrictive environment for learning. But the regular classroom is not the least restrictive environment for all students. For example, for an individual who is profoundly retarded, who is incontinent, and who needs one-to-one attention for most needs, mainstreaming would be outrageous. Similarly, for a psychotic child who needs a quiet, structured, controlled setting, the least restrictive environment would not be the regular classroom.

Reisman and Kauffman (1980) described steps in developing an IEP as follows:

a. documentation of the student's current level of educational performance;
b. annual goals expected to be attained by the end of the school year;
c. short-term objectives, stated in observable terms;
d. designation of special education and related services that will be provided to the child;
e. the extent of time the child will participate in the regular education program;
f. projected dates for initiating services and anticipated duration of these services; and
g. evaluation procedures and schedules for determining mastery of short-term objectives at least on an annual basis. (p. 214)

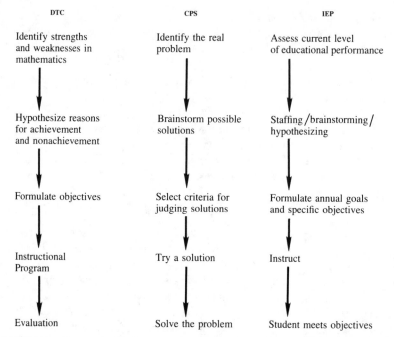

FIGURE 4 Comparison of Diagnostic Teaching Cycle (DTC), Creative Problem Solving (CPS), and Individual Education Plan (IEP)

The similarities among the Diagnostic Teaching Cycle, creative problem solving, and developing an IEP are illustrated in Figure 4.

At this time you might reread the major concerns listed on page 4. Awareness of these concerns is a first step in becoming a successful mathematics diagnostician. *Using* this awareness to incorporate ideas expressed by these concerns is a next step. In chapter 2, the Diagnostic Teaching Cycle is more fully explained. Application of the Diagnostic Teaching Cycle and use of creative problem solving will further your own growth as a mathematics teacher.

2

A Model for Diagnostic Teaching

The Diagnostic Teaching Cycle

Diagnostic teaching enables the teacher to determine what content is appropriate and how he or she can help the learner in the best way. The model of diagnostic teaching of elementary school mathematics shown in Figure 5 involves five processes:

1. Identifying the child's strengths and weaknesses in arithmetic performance
2. Hypothesizing possible reasons for these strengths and weaknesses
3. Formulating instructional objectives to serve as a structure for the enrichment of strengths or the remediation of weaknesses (see Mager, 1962; Popham & Baker, 1970)
4. Creating and trying corrective procedures (for further suggestions, see Glennon, 1963; Reisman, 1977, 1981; Reisman & Kauffman, 1980)
5. Ongoing evaluation of all phases of the diagnostic cycle to see if progress is being made in either alleviating trouble areas or in enriching strong areas.

Identifying

The *identification* process involves analyzing achievement test scores, scores on teacher-made tests, responses to mathematical problems during an interview by the teacher, or any other appropriate sample of the student's behavior. The identification component of diagnostic teaching depends upon

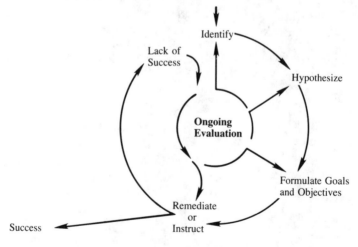

FIGURE 5 Diagnostic Teaching Cycle

the teacher's observation skills. It is important to be able to report what you observe. For example, to report that a student becomes flushed whenever mathematics lessons begin is an *observation*. On the other hand, to state that a student becomes anxious or ill during mathematics is an inference or a *hypothesis*. Observations are received through our senses. Inferences are interpretations and hypotheses about observations. Too often we jump to the inference too quickly—for example, "He hates math." "She's got 'math anxiety.'" "He's dumb." "She's shy." "She's bright but lazy."

A single observation may lead to several inferences. For example, take the case of the boy in gym class whose face had red blotches. The physical education teacher observed the red blotches and made a mental note to check it out. This teacher contacted the boy's homeroom teacher who also taught the language education class. The initial inferences by the physical education teacher were that the student was either coming down with some ailment or that he became flushed from physical activity. The homeroom teacher clarified the matter by explaining that the language education class was practicing a play about the circus and the red blotches were makeup for the clown part.

The distinction between observation and inference is the basic difference between the identification component and the hypothesizing part of the Diagnostic Teaching Cycle. The identification component utilizes observations from raw data such as test results, interviews, Piagetian tasks, and changes in physical appearance. Inferences are then made about these observations.

Hypothesizing

Once a student's areas of difficulty in learning mathematics have been identified, the *hypothesizing* function comes into play. What are possible reasons for the particular problems identified? Do diagnostic results indicate physical, cognitive, or emotional causes, or a combination of these? Do problems stem from the student's out-of-school environment, from his or her school experiences, or from intellectual and emotional concomitants? Usually a student's problems are not confined to a single cause. Human beings are complex animals and the causes of their problems are complex. The classroom diagnostician may have to deal with symptoms for an identification of the cause of a problem that is often elusive. Hypotheses serve as a structure to use in focusing attention on the relationship between symptoms and instructional procedures. Of course, inferences must be validated so as not to lead the teacher astray. The validation comes into play with use of both formative and summative evaluation. This point is emphasized throughout the explanation of the remainder of the diagnostic teaching model.

I tested a 10th-grade boy who was unable to multiply such a simple algebraic expression as $a(b + c)$. The boy scored in the above average range in intelligence, and diagnostic evidence indicated that he was well adjusted emotionally and socially. His work with whole numbers had been successful, and he was able to perform well with abstractions. In algebra, however, he was unable to multiply algebraic expressions. For example, he could not multiply $a(b+c)$ or $(a+b)(c+d)$, and he could not factor $(ab+ac)$. I hypothesized that the student's difficulty was in the cognitive domain and stemmed from a knowledge gap in his mathematical structure. It appeared that this boy needed to generalize the Distributive Property of Multiplication over Addition (DMPA) [for any three numbers a, b, and c, $a(b+c) = (ab+ac)$] from whole numbers to algebraic expressions. Since the boy was able to identify the distributive property with whole numbers in such an example as $7 \times 38 = 7 \times (30+8) = (7 \times 30) + (7 \times 8)$, I determined a carry-over to multiplying algebraic expressions would help. I found that he saw no connection between the distributive property in the above example with whole numbers and its use in multiplying algebraic expressions such as $a(b+c)$. Further inquiry showed that his algebra instruction had made no use of his whole number knowledge of the distributive property. This information led to instruction with more emphasis on meaning and a subsequent demand on his part to understand what he was doing. He was amazed to discover that $a(b+c)$ operated in the same way as 7×38. The following comparison table allowed him to see the step-by-step analogy:

	Arithmetic	*Algebra*
Step 1.	7×38	
Step 2.	$7 \times (30+8)$	$a(b+c)$
Step 3.	$(7 \times 30) \times (7 \times 8)$	$(a \times b) + (a \times c)$
Step 4.	$(210) + (56)$	$ab + ac$
Step 5.	266	

The renaming of the number 38 as the sum $30+8$ was compared to the sum $b+c$ in step 2. The distributive property was identified in step 3, and step 4 was said to involve the closure principle for multiplication. To help this boy with the concept of factoring, it was now a simple matter of reversing the above algebraic example as follows:

$$ab + ac$$

$$a(b+c)$$

The principle of identifying a common factor also was compared to whole number situations, and the student remarked that it was easier to identify the common factor in algebra since the letters kept their original name.

The comparison of common factors in both the number examples and the algebra examples served as a bridge for the student, which allowed him to proceed with algebra by using the DPMA in factoring algebraic expressions. Once he understood this relationship of the DPMA to algebraic operations, he then was able to perform in new situations employing the same axiom. The hypothesis that the boy needed guidance in applying the distributive property to algebraic expressions was verified by his success in working similar problems.

Formulating Goals and Objectives

The objective that served as the structure for the boy's instructional program was: To apply the Distributive Property of Multiplication over Addition to algebraic expressions. Both the content involved and the goal were included in the statement of the objective. The content dealt with the distributive property, and the goal was application of this content to a new and broader content: algebraic expressions. An instructional objective may be written in behavioral terms. A behavioral objective includes the concept or task to be learned and specifies what the child is to do that will show he or she has acquired a particular concept. Examples of other behavioral objectives and possible techniques of diagnosing whether the learner has attained them follow:

Objective. Complete equations to show the Commutative Property for Addition.

Diagnosis. Complete the following:

$$5+3=3+ \underline{\quad 5 \quad}$$
$$\square+0=0+ \underline{\quad \square \quad}$$
$$(4+5)+(9+7)=(9+7)+ \underline{(4+5)}$$
$$(4+5)+(9+7)=(7+9)+ \underline{(5+4)}$$

Objective. Show the Commutative Property for Addition with dot pictures.

Diagnosis. Complete the picture.

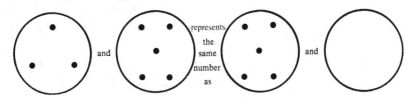

Objective. Identify the Commutative Property for Addition.

Diagnosis. Circle the letter for the Commutative Property for Addition.

$$a.\ 5 \times 3 = 3 + 5$$
$$b.\ 5 + 3 = 5 + 3$$
$$\boxed{c.}\ 5 + 3 = 3 + 5$$
$$d.\ (5 + 3) + 2 = 5 + (3 + 2)$$

Objective. Underline the step showing the Distributive Property for Multiplication over Addition.

Diagnosis.
$$7 \times 983 = 7 \times (900 + 80 + 3)$$
$$\underline{= (7 \times 900) + (7 \times 80) + (7 \times 3)}$$
$$= 6300 + 560 + 21$$
$$= 6881$$

Objective. Indicate examples of the Distributive Property for Multiplication over Addition.

Diagnosis. Circle the letter showing the Distributive Property of Multiplication over Addition.

$$a.\ \square + \triangle = \square$$
$$b.\ \square + \triangle = \square \times \triangle$$
$$c.\ (\square \times \triangle) + 0 = 0 + (\square \times \triangle)$$
$$\boxed{d.}\ \square(\triangle + 0) = (\square\triangle) + (\square 0)$$
$$e.\ (\square \times \triangle) + 0 = \square \times \triangle$$

Objective. Write a number as a product of its prime factors.

Diagnosis. Find the prime factors for the following numbers:

a. $32 = 2^5$

b. 14

$2 \cdot 7$

c. $36 = 2^2 \cdot 3^2$

d. $111 = 3 \cdot 37$

> Since the face value of the digits summed to 3, $1 + 1 + 1 = 3$, 111 was a multiple of 3.

e. 57

$3 \cdot 19$

> Since $5 + 7 = 12$, which is a multiple of 3, 57 is also a multiple of 3. For other divisibility rules see "Enrichment Mathematics for the Grades" (Glennon, 1963).

Remediating and Teaching

The *remediation* or *instructional* part of the diagnostic teaching cycle emerges from the other components. First, difficulties are identified; then their reasons for existing are hypothesized, and, finally, corrective procedures are undertaken.

Remediation can be either the most frustrating part of the diagnostic teaching model or its most gratifying concomitant. If the remediation yields successful performance on the part of the student who has been experiencing learning difficulties, the rewards are obvious. However, if the remedial procedures are ineffective, then the diagnostic cycle must be reinitiated and the processes of identification, formation of hypotheses, and formulation of objectives must be brought into operation again. New insights for the diagnostician may arise from the results of the remediation. Perhaps new areas of difficulty that are more closely related to the problem will be identified. These may not have been apparent in the original identification process. New hypotheses may arise that will prove to be more accurate than those already considered. Different behavioral objectives may also emerge from observing the learner's previous behavior.

The remediation component of the Diagnostic Teaching Cycle is instructional in nature. The diagnostic teacher must know the mathematics involved in such a way that he or she can determine what concepts the student needs to know in order to understand the mathematics that is a problem for the learner. The teacher must then be able to translate these prerequisite relationships into learning activities for the student. For example, consider a fifth grader who is having difficulty with addition of fractions with unlike denominators. The student could be tutored at the fifth-grade level of mathematics curriculum, but, more than likely, the remedial activities would need to be directed to lower level tasks such as finding the lowest common multiple (LCM) of two or more numbers; solving indirect open sentences for finding the appropriate name for the multiplicative identity; finding equivalent fractions by using the multiplicative identity; multiplying fractions; understanding the relation of denominator to numerator; drilling on basic addition and/or multiplication facts; or possibly understanding the cardinality of sets, since all of these ideas underlie adding fractions with unlike denominators. For example, what are some requisite objectives for the problem $\frac{2}{3} + \frac{1}{5}$?

Find the LCM to serve as the new denominator:

$$3, 6, 9, 12, \quad \fbox{15}$$
$$5, 10, \fbox{15} \qquad\qquad LCM = 15$$

Solve indirect open sentences to name the multiplicative identity:

$$3 \times \square = 15 \qquad 3 \times \boxed{5} = 15$$
$$5 \times \square = 15 \qquad 5 \times \boxed{3} = 15$$

Find equivalent fractions by using the multiplicative identity:

$$\frac{2}{3} \times \frac{\boxed{5}}{\boxed{5}} = \frac{}{15}$$

$$\frac{1}{5} \times \frac{\boxed{3}}{\boxed{3}} = \frac{}{15}$$

Multiply fractions:

$$\frac{2}{3} \times \frac{5}{5} = \frac{10}{15} \qquad\qquad \frac{2 \times 5}{3 \times 5} = \frac{10}{15}$$

or

$$\frac{1}{5} \times \frac{3}{3} = \frac{3}{15} \qquad\qquad \frac{1 \times 3}{5 \times 3} = \frac{3}{15}$$

Understand the relation of denominator to numerator:

$$\frac{10}{15}$$
$$+ \frac{3}{15}$$
$$\overline{}$$
$$\frac{13}{15} \quad and\ not\ \frac{13}{30}$$

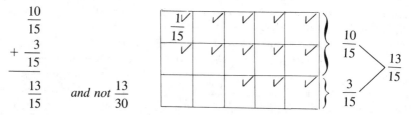

Drill on basic addition and/or multiplication facts:

$2 \times 5 = 10$	$0 + 3 = 3$
$3 \times 5 = 15$	$10 + 3 = 13$
$1 \times 3 = 3$	
$5 \times 3 = 15$	

Even though a student may be a fifth grader, he or she may have to analyze first-grade mathematics if this is the source of the mathematics weaknesses. Thus, the student's grade level in school is irrelevant; it is the level of knowledge of mathematical relations that determines the nature of the instructional program.

In addition, research beyond the classroom should investigate a child's cognitive style and way of learning. Thus far, our knowledge in these areas is minimal. Research on how children learn mathematical concepts needs to be coordinated with research dealing with anxiety and learning; knowledge in the areas of personality and perception should be investigated in terms of remedial techniques. Finally, research on the effects of malnutrition, diet, and other medical problems on intellectual development should be applied to learning mathematics.

Instruction may be considered as the verification function of the diagnostic cycle. Teachers should have in mind strategies for engaging in corrective procedures, and if some improvement is not apparent, they should reexamine their instructional program. If the original identification process led to hypothesizing that a more structured mathematics curriculum was needed, but, the student's performance became worse when this course was followed, the remediation program might be inappropriate, indeed, might even be harmful. I tested one child who initially was thought to be in need of in-depth mathematics instruction. However, when the results of psychological testing were considered, it was agreed that this child was in a highly anxious state and that a more effective remedial program would involve an easing-off on arithmetic involvement. The child had become the victim of a vicious cycle. His parents demanded high achievement in mathematics and became extremely tense when he did not meet their standards. Eventually, a pattern developed whereby the child became so tense during arithmetic tests, especially timed exams, that he would become physically ill. Thus, in this case, if a more stringent mathematics program had been undertaken, the emotional block to his learning of mathematics probably would have worsened. The frightening aspect of this case is that the boy had done such a good job of covering his anxiety that neither his parents nor his teacher had been aware of the extent to which it had developed until the physical symptoms became apparent. Effective remedial procedures included placing him in untimed situations when mathematics was involved, lessening demands for high achievement in mathematics, letting him know that he was loved and accepted with no strings (such as buying love with high achievement), and allowing him to team up with a friend in some test situations. The teacher reported that this idea of team test-taking led to a more relaxed test atmosphere for all of the students.

Evaluating

The ongoing nature of the fifth step in the Diagnostic Teaching Cycle, *evaluation*, is very important as a feedback function. If success emerges from the cycle, teachers will know that they are on the right track. A teacher evidently has identified the areas of weakness if a child who has previously had difficulty with a mathematical task or concept is now showing growth in this area.

The appropriateness of objectives that will emerge from components 1 and 2 of the Diagnostic Teaching Cycle is apparent in the degree of success the child displays in the remediation part of the cycle. If the instructional objectives were appropriate, then the child will display knowledge of the mathematics as a result of remediation.

Parts 1, 2, and 3 of the Diagnostic Teaching Cycle (identifying, hypothesizing, and formulating objectives) are quite interdependent. This triumvirate gives direction to the teaching phase of diagnosing by specifying content and techniques of instruction appropriate for a particular learner.

Evaluation of the program of remediation includes both cognitive and affective aspects. Do the children show evidence that they learned? Do they perform in an independent, happy, willing manner? Teachers should not be satisfied if only one of these conditions is met. For example, if a child now can solve mathematical sentences but appears hostile, anxious, or fatigued, this should be an indication of the need to formulate some corrective objectives in the affective domain.

Difficulties students encounter when they attempt to solve mathematical problems have been found to come from a number of conditions. Sometimes the nature of the mathematics problem has been misunderstood. A student's inability to comprehend the meaning of a problem might be associated with a weakness in reading ability. Misinterpreted directions may yield an unacceptable answer from the teacher's point of view, even though the answer would have been acceptable in light of the student's interpretation; for example, the teacher may accept 1/3 but not 2/6 or 12/36 as a correct response. Students may refuse to attempt any solution that appears abstract or complex because they are certain that it will be too difficult. This may indicate an inability on a child's part to transfer knowledge to a new problematic situation. Children may not have developed the necessary structure for planning an attack on a particular type of problem; they may lack necessary prerequisites for mathematical tasks because they were absent when a concept was taught, because they have forgotten it, or because they never learned it even though they were physically present. Diagnosis directs attention to such possibilities as well as to instances where children fail on purpose because of some need or emotional block. Emotional blocks are often the reason for bright children doing poorly in elementary school mathematics.

The evaluation process not only provides feedback to the teacher, but the learner also receives immediate reinforcement, which guides him or her to continue along the same route or to change course to accomplish an objective.

Analyzing a Skill to Be Learned

It is important to realize that diagnostic teaching is appropriate for all children: the gifted, the average, the slow learner, children who excel in mathematics, children who sometimes have difficulty with mathematics, and children who always are troubled by endeavors in mathematics. Diagnostic teaching encourages identification of new teaching sequences that are more effective with some children as well as allowing you to identify strong and weak areas in mathematics for one child or the whole class.

By analyzing a concept or skill to be taught, the teacher is in a position to set aside traditional teaching sequences and try new approaches. An example follows in regard to a time-telling sequence of instruction that was developed as a result of analyzing the task of telling time to the minute (Reisman, 1971). Not only did it become apparent that identifying time on a clock face was a skill rather than a time concept, but it also became clear that children could perform this skill before they had acquired the measurement of time concept. In fact, I found that some first graders could reproduce and identify time to the minute on a clock face, although it was not until third grade that children were responding correctly to the Piagetian "measurement of time" tasks (Piaget, 1966).

Jean Piaget (1966) has theorized that children's concepts of time and of duration depend on speed: ". . . one does not find that the young child has a concept of time which is radically independent of speed" (p. 208). Two different entities, succession of events and duration, are components of the notion of time. Succession of events refers to temporal order; duration is the interval between separate events. Piaget (1966) has discussed the ordinal notion of simultaneity, which he illustrates in the following experiment:

> We put two dolls on the table in front of the child and make them leave from the same place, side by side, and then stop beside one another. At the moments when they start and stop we make an audible click as a signal. We then ask the children if the dolls started at the same time or not, and whether they stopped at the same time or not. If the two moving dolls have the same speed and if they leave from the same place and stop at the same place, the children have no difficulty in telling that the dolls started and stopped at the same time. If, however, the speeds are changed so that the two dolls have the same starting point and the same stopping time but one of them reaches a more distant point, the results are different. All the children agree that the dolls started at the same time, that the departures are simultaneous. . . . They do not agree that the instants of arrival were simultaneous, for the moving dolls were not stopped at the same point.
>
> . . . "at the same time" is a phrase having no meaning for the young child. . . . "At the same time" has meaning only in the situation where the two dolls stayed next to each other throughout the entire trip. For movements of different velocities, with different points of arrival in space, simultaneity does not yet have significance because *the coordination of the time of one movement with the time of another movement presupposes a real understanding of the structure of time.*
>
> At about six years of age, while the child admits simultaneity, he does not yet conceive of the equality of synchronized durations. (The dolls) the child agrees . . . have left at the same time and . . . have stopped at the same time. But if . . .

asked whether one doll had moved for the same length of time as the other did
. . . reply is that one of them moved for a longer time because it has traveled
further.

. . . to make a comparison of movements through the same distances but at
different velocities one finds two distinct steps.

First, where the child replies "that one goes faster and [consequently] takes
more time": and afterwards, the child says, "that one is faster and [consequently]
takes less time." . . . *the first reply depends upon the result* (faster is equated with
farther and consequently with more time) and *the second upon* the process itself
(faster means less time). The second case, thus, expresses some operations which
bear on the transformation as such and not simply on the stationary result of
configuration (Piaget, 1966, pp. 208–309.)*

Piaget (1955) also used cars in place of dolls (p. 36). Believing cars to be
a less sex-bound stimulus than dolls, I used the following car tasks in a study
(Reisman, 1968).

Task 1. Both cars start at same place, travel at same speed, for the same
duration of time. They stop at same place.

$$X — — — — \; X$$
$$X — — — — \to X$$

Task 2. Both cars start at same place, travel at different speeds, and for
the same duration of time. They stop at different places.

$$X — — \; X$$
$$X— \longrightarrow X$$

Task 3. Both cars start at same place, travel at same speeds, and for
different durations of time. They stop at different places.

$$X— \to X$$
$$X— — \to X$$

Task 2 was the crucial activity so far as the system of time measurement is
concerned because the measurement of time is dependent upon the understanding of the "coordination of operations of temporal succession and time
duration" (Reisman, 1968, p. 163).

Prior to that time nothing is gained by the utilization of a watch . . . because the
small child of four to six years does not understand that the speed of movement of

---

*From "Time Perception in Children" by Jean Piaget. In *The Voices of Time,* edited by
J. T. Fraser (New York: George Braziller, 1966; London: Penguin Books, 1966). Reprinted by
permission.

hands on a watch is constant. For example, if the child observes a watch in order to estimate the time taken by an object to execute a rapid movement, the hand of the watch appears to him to move more slowly than if he tries to estimate the time taken by an object in slower motion . . . the child sees no reason why he should assume that the rate of displacement of the watch hand . . . is constant. He has not yet the intellectual tools to understand the problem of conservation of speed. . . . The development of systematic time concepts is . . . at no point independent of the understanding of concepts of speed. (Piaget, 1955, p. 41)*

According to Piaget (1955), success on Task 2 does not occur before the ages of seven or eight:

> . . . Let us consider the situation in which two moving bodies start simultaneously from the same point: B moving more rapidly than A has covered more distance at the moment of simultaneous arrest. Here, children of approximately four to six years of age admit without difficulty the simultaneity of departure but not that of arrest. Yet, this is not due to any perceptual errors. The subject acknowledges easily that when B stops, A no longer moves, and vice versa. He refuses to say, however, that the objects came to rest at the same time, "together." The child thinks B stopped "before" A because the former is "ahead" of the latter in the spatial sense; or else he thinks that A stopped before B stopped "first" in the sense that it is spatially closer. . . . In summary it can be said that, at the "preoperative" level of development, the child's judgments of simultaneity or successiveness in time depend on the equality or inequality of the speed of objects moving along the same path. (pp. 36–37).*

Although first graders could reproduce and identify time on a clock face, which are skills, most of the third graders did not have the concepts necessary for an *understanding* of time measurement (Reisman, 1968).

Once you analyze a concept or skill into its parts and rearrange these in a sequence of instruction, you may enter the resulting instructional program according to the particular needs of the child. Following is a suggested instructional sequence for teaching the skill of identifying time on a clock face.

Time-telling Objectives

1. To say the names of the numerals from 1 to 12.
2. To identify the numerals 1 to 12.
3. To count to 60 by ones using a number line.

---

*From "The Development of Time Concepts in the Child" by Jean Piaget. In *Psychopathology of Childhood,* edited by Paul Hoch and Joseph Lubin (New York: Grune and Stratton, 1955). Reprinted by permission.

4. To recognize that the 60 numerals on a number line match up in a one-to-one correspondence with the 60-minute marks on a clock face.

5. To recognize that the circumference of a clock face is like a number line that is curved.

6. To recognize that the longer minute hand is the pointer for the ''60'' number line.

7. To count clockwise by ones every minute mark from the zero mark on a clock face to determine the number of minutes after an hour indicated by the longer pointer.

8. To say ''_____ minutes after'' the hour.

9. To place the numerals 1 to 12 in order on a number line and then count them aloud.

10. To move the numerals 1 to 12 from their number line position to their clock face position.

11. To read aloud all of the numerals on a clock face in a clockwise direction starting at 12.

12. To recognize relationship between the placement of numerals on the ''12'' number line and the multiples of five on the ''60'' number line when both number lines are of the same length.

13. To map the multiples of five on the ''60'' number line onto the ''12'' number line in a counting sequence using the idea of many-to-one relation.

14. To keep a tally on the ''12'' number line the number of times one counts to 60 on the ''60'' number line.

15. To recognize that the tally counter on the ''12'' number line is doing the same job as the hour hand on the clock face.

16. To show zero minutes after the hour with the minute pointer.

17. To say ''o'clock'' when the minute hand is at the top center position pointing to the ''12'' on the clock face.

18. To read _____:00 as o'clock.

19. To recognize that the minute hand (longer pointer) points to the top center of the clock face when the clock reads _____:00.

20. To associate the word o'clock with ''_____:00'' and the top center position of the minute hand.

21. To associate hours with the numeral indicated by the shorter hour hand on the clock face.

22. To determine the hour as indicated by the numeral that the hour hand is pointing to when the minute hand is pointing to the top center of the clock face.

23. To recognize that the longer hand is always pointing to the numeral 12 when the hour hand points directly to a numeral on the clock face.

24. To show a designated time on the clock face; time designated will be time on the hour.
25. To read aloud the time as indicated by the positions of the hands for time on the hour.
26. To say "o'clock" when reading or referring to time on the hour.
27. To identify time on the hour.
28. To recognize that the hour hand moves slowly from one numeral to the next in relation to the movement of the minute hand.
29. To tell time correctly to the minute using the language "after the hour."
30. To recognize that 30 minutes after the hour is the same as (is another name for) "half after the hour."
31. To say "half after the hour."
32. To show time on the half hour.
33. To identify time on the half hour.
34. To say the minutes and hours in sequence, "31 minutes after 7."
35. To count by fives on the "60" number line.
36. To count by fives on a clock face using the numerals one to twelve on the clock face as a guide.
37. To count multiples of five on a clock face as indicated by the numeral on the clock face to which the longer hand is pointing.
38. To say the minutes and hours in sequence when the minutes are multiples of five, "20 minutes after 4" or "45 minutes after 11."
39. To tell time to the minute using the language after the hour with facility by counting first by fives and then by ones until the position of the minute hand is reached.   .
40. To recognize that 15 minutes after the hour is another name for a quarter after the hour, and that 30 minutes after is another name for half after the hour.
41. To say "a quarter after the hour."
42. To recognize that 45 minutes after the hour is another name for three-quarters after the hour.
43. To recognize that three-quarters after the hour is another name for a quarter before the next hour.
44. To recognize that another name for a quarter before the next hour is 15 minutes before the next hour.
45. To recognize that 45 minutes after one hour is another name for 15 minutes before the next hour.
46. To use the language "after the hour" when referring to the number of minutes the minute hand has traveled past the numeral 12 on a clock face, and use the language "before the hour" when referring to the number of minutes the minute hand must travel to reach the numeral 12 again during a span of 60 minutes.

47. To count in a clockwise direction the number of minutes the minute hand must traverse to reach the numeral 12.
48. To count in a counterclockwise direction from the numeral 12 to determine how many minutes the minute hand must travel before it will reach the numeral 12.
49. To tell time to the minute using the language "*n* minutes after the hour," "*n* minutes before the hour," "¼ after," "½ after," and "¼ before."
50. To show the correct time on a clock face in response to the language "*n* minutes after," "*n* minutes before," "¼ after," "½ after," "¼ before," when these times are spoken.
51. To show the correct time on a clock face in response to the written forms: "8:00, 8:16, a quarter after 8, a quarter to nine, 8:30, half after 8, 8:45, 8:53."
52. To draw the hands on a clock face to show designated times.
53. To show time on a clock face expressed in writing.
54. To identify the time shown on a clock face by selecting the correct written response from a set of pictures of clocks.

Another example of a change in the usual sequence of instruction occurs in the teaching of multiplication of fractions prior to the teaching of addition of fractions. For years, children were expected to add fractions with unlike denominators before they had instruction in those concepts prerequisite to the task at hand. However, upon analyzing the concepts involved, it is apparent that the child who cannot rename 2/3 as 4/6 will not be able to add 2/3 + 1/2. The child must be able to find common denominators and rename equivalent fractions in order to add fractions with unlike denominators.

When you, the teacher, analyze a mathematical task into its parts and reflect on some of your students' errors in performing the particular task, you are gathering information that will help you to mesh the sequence of these parts with the child's rate of cognitive development and with the child's optimal way of learning in terms of concrete, picture, or symbolic representation of concepts and/or relationships involved.

PART 2

Assessment Instruments and Procedures

The identification component of the Diagnostic Teaching Cycle (DTC) relies upon selection of relevant assessments and knowledgeable use of the results of these assessments. Test instruments and procedures such as Piagetian tasks must be selected in relation to the phenomenon being assessed. In other words, the identification tools must be valid. Furthermore, if a standardized test is used, then teachers must adhere to the administration and scoring instructions as published. The strength of the identification component of the DTC is dependent upon the extent to which the test items tap the goals of the instructional program. Teachers should be aware of the importance of going beyond standardized test results in diagnosing class performance. Standardized tests are noted for shallow coverage of content in order to gain broad coverage of instructional objectives. Thus criterion-referenced teacher-made tests should be used to supplement the standardized or norm-referenced tests.

After identifying individual or class strengths and weaknesses, inferences about assessment results form the basis for hypotheses about causes of learning problems and how to avoid or alleviate them.

Teachers must be aware of the psychological aspects of curriculum. Teachers must be concerned with questions regarding cognitive processes involved, e.g., Is an arbitrary fact to be learned? Is a relation, a concept, or a generalization to be constructed?

Questions related to emotional aspects of learning also must be considered, e.g., Are a low-self-concept and/or unfilled human needs inhibiting

37

mathematics performance? The results of the hypothesizing component of the DTC provides information for instructional goals and strategies. Teachers must be made aware of the link between assessment and instruction. The DTC is a model that makes apparent the relationship between testing, evaluation, and instruction.

3

Norm-referenced Tests

Unfortunately, most classroom teachers usually have little to say about the selection of standardized tests. However, when teachers *are* involved, these important questions should be addressed:

1. To what degree are our students reflected in the norming population?
2. To what extent is our curriculum represented in the test objectives?
3. To what extent is what we actually do in the classroom reflected in the test items?

In regard to the first question teachers need to know if the level of language is appropriate, if directions are given in ways that students are used to, if time limits are sufficient for students' abilities, and if test formats are familiar to the students. Question two suggests that the majority of content of the test items must be the same as that which is taught in the classroom of the teacher administering the test. Consideration of question three helps to ensure that there is a parallel between classroom instruction and standardized testing. Many times students are given a great deal of instruction at the concrete level and are tested only at the paper-pencil level. Thus, test items should include concrete tasks and use of pictures as well as symbols.

Types of Tests

Before selecting and/or using the various types of standardized tests, teachers need to become familiar with terms related to norm-referenced tests, the most important of which are described as follows:

Norms refer to average performance of a group upon which individual performance may be judged.

Norm-referenced tests are tests in which student performance is interpreted in terms of norms.

Standardized tests rely upon empirical data obtained from administrations to defined samples under specific conditions (e.g., instructions for administration including time limits and scoring criteria).

Teachers also need to know the differences among various types of tests. Jensen (1980) has distinguished among various types of tests and has helped to clarify the confusion that often arises about test terms, namely, aptitude or intelligence, achievement, assessment, and diagnostic.

Aptitude or Intelligence Tests

Many people claim that intelligence or *aptitude* tests are achievement tests. This is because aptitude tests include tasks that are comprised of information and skills that had to be learned, e.g., vocabulary, information items, solutions to arithmetic problems. Furthermore, all tests involve performance, and "*all* performance is a form of achievement" (Jensen, 1980, p. 239).

However, there are some distinguishing features between *aptitude* and *achievement* tests, which can be summarized as follows:

In terms of *sampling,* aptitude tests are broader and more heterogeneous and are based upon a wider set of experiences. Achievement tests sample specifiic knowledge and skills related to formal schooling.

In terms of *time,* aptitude tests sample cumulated knowledge and skills from all times in past experience. Achievement tests tap acquisitions from the recent past as at the end of a course or year in school. In terms of *test items,* aptitude tests involve many types of items involving some complexity. Achievement test items are task specific.

In terms of *function,* aptitude tests are used for prediction of future intellectual achievements. Achievement tests are used to evaluate what has been learned.

In terms of *stability,* aptitude tests are less susceptible to the effects of instruction across time than are achievement tests. Achievement test results are *influenced* by aptitude, motivation and opportunity. (Jensen, 1980, p. 239)

When individuals have the same experiences, for example, natural brothers and sisters reared together, "there is such a high correlation between intelligence test scores and scholastic achievement as to make the two kinds of scores operationally indistinguishable" (Jensen, 1980, p. 240). When there are differences in experiences, opportunities, motivation, or lack of social sanctions against poor performance, the correlation between performance on aptitude and achievement tests is lower. Jensen (1980) pointed out that "for short-term prediction, the individual's recent past achievement is, generally, the best predictor of his or her achievement in the near future" (p. 241).

Achievement Tests

When selecting an achievement test, teachers should inquire of the publisher about the population for which the test was designed to insure its appropriateness to their students. The mathematics content of the test should be examined to determine that it is testing appropriate mathematics curriculum for the children involved. Following are some published achievement tests that include mathematics subtests:

California Achievement Tests
Metropolitan Achievement Tests
SRA Reading and Arithmetic Indexes
Stanford Achievement Test
Wide Range Achievement Test

The Seventh Mental Measurements Yearbook (Buros, 1972) can provide useful information and help you to evaluate the various published achievement tests.

Assessment Tests

Assessment tests measure the results of training or educational programs and in this sense may include achievement tests. Assessment tests are also pretests—tests that are given at the beginning of a course and that are used to provide baseline data for evaluating (a) training versus prior attainment, (b) mastery in course content, or (c) effectiveness of different methods of instruction.

Assessment tests are only as effective as their content validity. Content validity refers to the match between the test items' content and the knowledge or skills to which the training was directed.

An annotated list of many of the published mathematics assessment tests is presented below.

> Connolly, A. J.; Nachtman, W.; & Pritchett, E. M., *Key Math Diagnostic Arithmetic Test*. American Guidance Service, Inc., Circle Pines, Minnesota. 1971.
>
> *Fountain Valley Teacher Support System in Mathematics.* Richard L. Zweig Associates, Inc., 20800 Beach Boulevard, Huntington Beach, California 92648. 1972.
>
> May, L. J.; & Hood, V., *BASE (Basic Arithmetic Skill Evaluation)*. Media Research Associates, 1735 23rd Street S.E., Salem, Oregon 97302. 1973.
>
> *Noonan-Spradley Diagnostic Program of Computational Skills.* Allied Education Council Distribution Center, P.O. Box 78, Galien, Michigan 49113. 1970.
>
> Reisman, F. *Sequential Assessment in Mathematics Instruction (SAMI).* Charles E. Merrill Publishing Co., Columbus, Ohio. In press.
>
> *Stanford Diagnostic Arithmetic Tests.* Harcourt, Brace, and World, Inc., New York, New York. 1966. (Level 1 is intended for grade 2 to grade 4; Level 2 is for grade 4 through grade 8.)
>
> *Stanford Early School Achievement Test.* Harcourt, Brace, Jovanovich, Inc., New York, New York. 1969. (Level 1 is intended for kindergarten and beginning grade 1.)
>
> *A Test of Understandings of Selected Properties of a Number System: Primary Form.* Indiana University Bureau of Educational Studies and

Testing, Bloomington, Indiana. Bulletin of the School of Education. 1966. (For children in grades 1 and 2.)

Welch, R. C.; & Edwards, C. W., *A Test of Arithmetic Principles: Elementary Form*. Indiana University Bureau of Educational Studies and Testing, Bloomington, Indiana. Bulletin of the School of Education. 1965. (For children eight years old and older.)

Diagnostic Tests

Diagnosis comes into play when assessment reveals a deviation from the class average or some "norm." Diagnosis is an attempt to understand causes of these deviations from average performance, usually when assessment results indicate progress that is not consistent with aptitude—especially when an individual's achievement is at least one year below what is expected in terms of his or her aptitude test performance.

Diagnostic tests may or may not have content validity relevant to the knowledge and skills to be developed in a particular course. Jensen (1980) described this phenomenon:

> Diagnostic tests may have content validity relevant to the subject matter of the course, but they need not have content validity. Tests of other abilities or traits that are correlated with achievement may be useful for diagnosis. Special tests devised to measure fine-grained components of the course content, such as visual acuity, form perception, and eye movements, in the case of reading, may yield helpful information. So may tests of prerequisite knowledge or skills. Most often tests of general ability or IQ tests are used in diagnosis, with the rationale that such tests reflect the subject's achievements in a much broader sphere and thus may be indicative of his typical capacity for learning. (p. 45)

The Piagetian tasks described in Chapter 6 are examples of normative diagnostic items that do not have content validity for specific arithmetical tasks, such as computation. However, they are related to ability to construct such mathematical knowledge as *one-to-one correspondence* (e.g., match a number of cowboys with a number of horses), *seriation* (e.g., arrange a number of straws of different lengths in order from shortest to longest), *classification* (e.g., place a pile of white and black buttons, of large, medium, and small size into either two groups by color or three groups by size), and *conservation* (see pp. 88–90). Pinard and Laurendau (1964) and Goldschmidt and Bentler (1968a, 1968b) have provided normed Piagetian tasks that can be used for diagnostic purposes.

How to Use a Standardized Mathematics Assessment

According to the model of diagnostic teaching, teachers—not tests—are considered diagnostic. Tests are to be considered as tools for observing student performance. When considering a classroom of children, it must be assumed that for various reasons, each child is performing at a different level of mathematical thinking. Consider two members of a class who miss the same item for different reasons. These underlying causes hold the key for instruction, and this kind of information is not always apparent from the tests results. It is impossible to construct a test that taps the total range of a mathematics curriculum and that provides information as to why a child misses one item and has answered the preceding item correctly. An analysis of published tests that purport to be diagnostic shows that between most items, several missing relations and concepts may exist. Furthermore, most tests do not provide enough information as to *why* a child has answered an item or group of items incorrectly. Is the mode (not to be confused with modality) of response preventing the child from correctly answering an item, or is the difficulty due to lack of a mathematics concept or skill? Attention must be given the type of expressive behavior that is called for, as well as to the nature of the curriculum to be learned. Therefore, the diagnostic teacher must analyze and interpret the child's performance in light of these issues in order to guard against erroneous conclusions.

Testing for a student's knowledge of concepts that come between items on these grosser measures is by no means a simple task. However, it must be done, and by the regular classroom teacher whenever possible, to insure an effective instructional program in mathematics. This means that the teacher of elementary school mathematics needs to know the mathematics content of at least eighth-grade level. In this regard, many college students have been upset with their lack of mathematics knowledge. Students expressing such concerns should select one area, probably the topic most pressing for their immediate arithmetic teaching needs, and study this in depth for a year. Repeat the procedure using a different topic each year, and at the end of five years, the individual will have learned five topics that he or she must teach. This strategy is more productive than simply being angry at oneself about a lack of mathematics knowledge.

A diagnostic teacher must be able to analyze the mathematics curriculum in order to develop instructional sequences that will fill gaps in a student's mathematical foundation. Protocols must be developed for identifying strengths and weaknesses of a student or group of students that include concrete and picture tasks as well as paper-pencil tests. The results of such assessment may be used as a guide to diagnostic testing in the form of "teacher-made diagnostic tests" that are designed to tap those gaps that are inherent in most published tests.

Diagnostic testing and teaching may be used as a strategy for organizing the classroom into instructional groups. The published assessment tests are a helpful first step in accomplishing flexible grouping techniques. For example, after a standardized mathematics survey has been administered, list the members of your class and record the grade score for those students who have scored below grade level. The grade score for each raw score can be found in the test manual that accompanies the published test.

The grade score (or grade equivalent) refers to the average performance of a group of pupils at a particular grade level. A grade score of 58 (or grade equivalent of 5.8) refers to the average achievement of pupils in the eighth month of the fifth grade. By looking up the grade score that corresponds to a specific raw score (the actual score that a pupil makes on the test), you can tell if the student is above, below, or at his or her actual grade placement.

For example, if a test is administered to a sixth-grade class in October, this would be an actual grade placement of 6.2 (they are in the sixth year of school, and October is the second month of the school year). If a student's raw score is converted to a grade score by means of the conversion tables found in the test manuals for standardized tests and is found to be 6.0, the student's achievement is slightly below that of the typical student in grade 6.2 (see the section on *how to identify the underachiever* on pp. 46–52).

A weak area is determined by converting the student's total score on the test to a grade score. Those areas that show grade scores one year or more below the actual grade level should be investigated. This type of class survey summary may be used to identify areas in which the entire class is weak, as well as to identify those students weak in a specific area.

A suggested form for a survey summary for a fifth-grade, sixth-month (5.6) class follows. (See p. 160 in Appendix E for an alternate format.)

Class Survey Summary

*Date of Testing*_____   *Test Administered*_____

Name	*Arithmetic Computation*	*Arithmetic Concepts*	*Arithmetic Application*
Allen, Mary			
Brown, John			3.8
Crown, Joe			
McCarthy, Helen		4.3	
Michaels, Jon			4.4

Class Survey Summary—*continued*

Name	Arithmetic Computation	Arithmetic Concepts	Arithmetic Application
Olive, Carol			4.5
Peters, Sue			3.7
Roberts, Sam	4.6		
Rollins, Jack			4.4
Sullivan, Tom		4.6	
Tompson, Jan		4.4	3.9
Victor, Marie			4.5
Williams, Joe			
Wilson, Sue			
Young, Tony	4.4	4.6	3.9
Zellin, Marge			
Zen, Chien			
Zepher, Keith			

A glance at the class chart of 18 students shows that eight students, or 44 percent of the class, had grade scores of at least one grade level below their present grade placement in Arithmetic Application, which includes verbal problem solving. If the rest of the class scored around grade level or only a little higher on this part, there would be evidence that the methods of teaching verbal problem solving in this particular class needs evaluating.

Those four students showing a weakness in Arithmetic Concepts can be identified easily, as can the two students needing help in computation.

How to Identify the Underachiever—Interpreting Grade Equivalents

Very seldom is it enough to look at a child's grade equivalent score on a standardized achievement test to decide whether or not he or she is an underachiever. Since all children do not have the same intellectual capacity, a grade placement score may mean one thing for one child and something entirely different for another. For this reason, it is helpful to be able to determine the child's expected grade equivalent (XGE) based on intellectual capacity.

Let us assume that a nine-year-old (actually nine years and eight months) child is in the third month of grade four (4.3), has an IQ of 140, and has a mathematics achievement test score of 7.0. The fact that he is in 4.3 grade and has obtained a grade placement score of 7.0 appears to be outstanding. However, in computing his *expected* grade equivalent score, we find this to be 7.4. Thus, he is achieving at a level that is to be expected when considering his high IQ.

Now let us consider another child, also in grade 4.3 and also aged 9.8. However, this child's IQ is 76 and his score on the same mathematics achievement test was 3.1. It appears that this student is not achieving to his fullest. But, when you account for his performance on the test of intellectual ability, you find that he is achieving pretty much at the level to be expected since his XGE is approximately 3.3. For a child to be considered an under-achiever, a rule-of-thumb interpretation is that his grade equivalent scores on normed tests should be ten or more months below his expected grade equivalent score obtained from his performance on tests of mental power that are appropriate to the child's culture and presented in his most facile language. In our hypothetical case, this was not true since the student's mathematics score was only two months below his XGE.

Here are the steps for finding the XGE score:

1. Find the child's IQ. Tests such as the Slosson Intelligence Test for Children and Adults (Slosson, 1968) or the Peabody Picture Vocabulary Test (Dunn, 1965) do not require special training as do the Wechsler Intelligence Scale for Children–Revised (WISC–R) (Weschler, 1974) or the Stanford-Binet Intelligence Scale Manual for the Third Revision, Form L-M (Terman & Merrill, 1962).
2. Identify the child's present age (CA or chronological age) and grade in school.
3. Find the child's expected grade equivalent by referring to the *Expectancy Scores Table* on pp. 48–50.* Find the appropriate number in the IQ column; then move horizontally until you come to the most appropriate age/grade column for the child. Read the XGE from the table, or perform the necessary computations within the table as shown in the examples that follow.

The *Expectancy Scores Table* presents estimates of expected grade equivalents. For example, the approximate XGE for a child who is 8.5 years old with an IQ of 93 is 3.2. This may be found by subtracting the XGE for age eight (2.8) from the XGE for age nine (3.6), finding half of this difference (.4), and adding this to the age eight score ($2.8 + .4 = 3.2$).

Take the example of a child of 11 years and 3 months (11.3). Since the table includes only scores for even ages, some computation will be necessary to find XGEs for years and months. On p. 51 is a step-by-step procedure for finding XGEs for ages other than $+ .5$ of a year, as was shown in the above example.

---

*Appreciation is expressed to Colleen Hartley, special education teacher, Riverside, California, for identifying a need for the Expectancy Scores Table, and to Joe Hartley, Esq., for producing the computer program and printout of the table.

Expectancy Scores

I Q	*Grades* 1 (Age 6–0)	2 (Age 7–0)	3 (Age 8–0)	4 (Age 9–0)	5 (Age 10–0)	6 (Age 11–0)	7 (Age 12–0)	8 (Age 13–0)
70	K.1	1.0	1.8	2.4	3.0	3.8	4.3	5.1
71	K.2	1.0	1.9	2.4	3.1	3.9	4.4	5.2
72	K.2	1.1	1.9	2.5	3.1	3.9	4.5	5.3
73	K.2	1.0	2.0	2.5	3.2	4.0	4.6	5.4
74	K.3	1.1	2.0	2.6	3.3	4.1	4.7	5.5
75	K.3	1.2	2.0	2.7	3.4	4.2	4.8	5.6
76	K.3	1.2	2.1	2.7	3.4	4.2	4.9	5.7
77	K.4	1.2	2.1	2.8	3.5	4.4	5.0	5.8
78	K.3	1.2	2.1	2.8	3.6	4.4	5.1	5.9
79	K.4	1.3	2.2	2.9	3.6	4.5	5.2	6.0
80	K.4	1.3	1.2	2.9	3.7	4.6	5.2	6.1
81	K.4	1.3	2.2	3.0	3.7	4.6	5.3	6.2
82	K.5	1.4	2.3	3.0	3.8	4.7	5.4	6.3
83	K.5	1.5	2.4	3.1	3.9	4.8	5.5	6.4
84	K.6	1.5	2.4	3.1	3.9	4.8	5.6	6.5
85	K.6	1.5	2.4	3.2	4.0	4.9	5.7	6.6
86	K.6	1.6	2.5	3.2	4.1	5.0	5.7	6.6
87	K.7	1.6	2.5	3.3	4.1	5.0	5.8	6.7
88	K.7	1.6	2.6	3.6	4.2	5.1	5.9	6.8
89	K.7	1.7	2.6	3.4	4.3	5.2	6.0	6.9
90	K.7	1.7	2.6	3.5	4.4	5.3	6.1	7.0
91	K.8	1.7	2.7	3.5	4.4	5.3	6.2	7.2
92	K.8	1.8	2.7	3.6	4.5	5.5	6.3	7.3
93	K.8	1.8	2.8	3.6	4.6	5.5	6.4	7.4
94	K.9	1.8	2.8	3.7	4.6	5.6	6.5	7.5

Expectancy Scores—(cont.)

I Q	Grades 1 (Age 6–0)	2 (Age 7–0)	3 (Age 8–0)	4 (Age 9–0)	5 (Age 10–0)	6 (Age 11–0)	7 (Age 12–0)	8 (Age 13–0)
95	K.9	1.9	2.8	3.7	4.7	5.7	6.6	7.6
96	K.9	1.9	2.9	3.8	4.7	5.7	6.6	7.6
97	1.0	1.9	2.9	3.8	4.8	5.8	6.7	7.7
98	1.0	1.9	2.9	3.9	4.9	5.9	6.8	7.8
99	1.0	2.0	3.0	3.9	4.9	5.9	6.9	7.9
100	1.0	2.0	3.0	4.0	5.0	6.0	7.0	8.0
101	1.0	2.0	3.0	4.1	5.1	6.1	7.1	8.1
102	1.1	2.1	3.1	4.1	5.1	6.1	7.2	8.2
103	1.1	2.2	3.2	4.2	5.2	6.2	7.3	8.3
104	1.2	2.2	3.2	4.2	5.3	6.3	7.4	8.4
105	1.2	2.2	3.2	4.3	5.4	6.4	7.5	8.5
106	1.2	2.3	3.3	4.3	5.4	6.4	7.6	8.6
107	1.3	2.3	3.3	4.4	5.5	6.6	7.7	8.7
108	1.3	2.3	3.4	4.4	5.6	6.6	7.8	8.8
109	1.3	2.4	3.4	4.5	5.6	6.7	7.9	8.9
110	1.3	2.4	3.4	4.5	5.7	6.8	7.9	9.0
111	1.4	2.4	3.5	4.6	5.7	6.8	8.0	9.1
112	1.4	2.5	3.5	4.6	5.8	6.9	8.1	9.2
113	1.4	2.5	3.6	4.7	5.9	7.0	8.2	9.3
114	1.5	2.5	3.6	4.8	5.9	7.0	8.3	9.4
115	1.5	2.6	3.6	4.8	6.0	7.1	8.4	9.5
116	1.5	2.6	3.7	4.9	6.1	7.2	8.5	9.6
117	1.6	2.6	3.7	4.9	6.1	7.2	8.6	9.7
118	1.5	2.6	3.7	5.0	6.2	7.3	8.7	9.8
119	1.6	2.7	3.8	5.0	6.3	7.4	8.8	9.9

Expectancy Scores—(cont.)

I Q	Grades 1 (Age 6–0)	2 (Age 7–0)	3 (Age 8–0)	4 (Age 9–0)	5 (Age 10–0)	6 (Age 11–0)	7 (Age 12–0)	8 (Age 13–0)
120	1.6	2.7	3.8	5.1	6.4	7.5	8.8	9.9
121	1.6	2.7	3.8	5.1	6.4	7.5	8.9	10.1
122	1.7	2.8	3.9	5.2	6.5	7.7	9.0	10.2
123	1.7	2.9	4.0	5.2	6.6	7.7	9.1	10.3
124	1.8	2.9	4.0	5.3	6.6	7.8	9.2	10.4
125	1.8	2.9	4.0	5.4	6.7	7.9	9.3	10.5
126	1.8	3.0	4.1	5.4	6.7	7.9	9.3	10.5
127	1.9	3.0	4.1	5.5	6.8	8.0	9.4	10.6
128	1.9	3.0	4.2	5.5	6.9	8.1	9.5	10.7
129	1.9	3.1	4.2	5.6	6.9	8.1	9.6	10.8
130	1.9	3.1	4.2	5.6	7.0	8.2	9.7	10.9
131	2.0	3.1	4.3	5.7	7.1	8.3	9.8	11.1
132	2.0	3.2	4.3	5.7	7.1	8.3	9.9	11.2
133	2.0	3.2	4.4	5.8	7.2	8.4	10.0	11.3
134	2.1	3.2	4.4	5.8	7.3	8.5	10.1	11.4
135	2.1	3.3	4.4	5.9	7.4	8.6	10.2	11.5
136	2.1	3.3	4.5	5.9	7.4	8.6	10.2	11.5
137	2.2	3.3	4.5	6.0	7.5	8.8	10.3	11.6
138	2.1	3.3	4.5	6.1	7.6	8.8	10.4	11.7
139	2.2	3.4	4.6	6.1	7.6	8.9	10.5	11.8
140	2.2	3.4	4.6	6.2	7.7	9.0	10.6	11.9

Child's Age	IQ	Range of Child's Age	Range of Child's XGE	Child's XGE*
11.3	119	11.0–12.0	7.4–8.8	7.8

*a. Find difference of range of child's XGE in table $(8.8 - 7.4 = 1.4)$.
  b. Multiply this difference by the number of months expressed in tenths of a year above the lower limit of the Range of Child's Age in table $(.3 \times 1.4 = .42)$.
  c. Add this product to the lower limit of the Range of Child's XGE in table $(7.4 + .42 = 7.82$ or $7.8)$. Therefore, the XGE for a child who is 11.3 years of age with an IQ of 119 is 7.8. Steps a, b, and c may also be used to find the XGE for $+ .5$ of a year.

The Expectancy Scores Table was based upon the following formulas devised by Horn (1941).

Child's Present Age	Horn's Formula
6.0–8.5	$\dfrac{MA + CA}{2}$
8.6–9.11	$\dfrac{3\,MA + 2CA}{5}$
10.0–11.11	$\dfrac{2MA + CA}{3}$
12 and above	$\dfrac{3MA + CA}{4}$

NOTE: For those wishing to compute XGEs, convert the child's age (CA) to months in the IQ formula for finding his mental age (MA), by using the form $12 \times y + m,$ where $y = $ years and $m = $ months.

Example: If 7.1 means seven years and one month,
        then $12 \times 7 + 1 = 85$ months.

Example: If 7.10 means seven years and ten months,
        then $12 \times 7 + 10 = 84 + 10 = 94$ months.

    In the following chart, Mary, John, and Phillip are underachievers as shown by the expected grade equivalents (XGE) for each child. These computations have been done as additional examples for the reader.

Child	IQ	Age	Grade Score on Achievement Test	XGE	Under-achiever
Mary	131	8.6	3.2	5.1	√
June	123	8.6	3.9	4.7	
Bill	89	10.7	4.0	4.9	
John	115	7.2	1.7	2.8	√
Phillip	108	10.2	4.2	5.8	√

The next step after analyzing the results of a standardized mathematics test is to sample content in the troubled areas in depth. At this point you may want to build your own informal assessments that are tailored to sample concepts which occur between items on the standardized published test.

4

Criterion-referenced Tests

Criterion-referenced tests measure performance as compared to specified and required levels of mastery. For example, on the mathematics assessment (SAMI) presented in the next chapter, the student must obtain 80 percent of the test items correct to meet criterion performance on each part of the test. Criterion-referenced tests are developed from sequences of instructional objectives based upon task analyses of broad instructional goals. Teacher-made diagnostic assessments may be classified as criterion-referenced tests.

Teacher-made Diagnostic Tests

Teacher-made diagnostic tests may take the form of checklists, paper-pencil tests, interviews, or observation of children engaged in activities at the concrete, picture, and symbolic levels. For example, in the time-telling instructional sequence, detailed earlier, a simple *checklist* of the 54 objectives can quickly reflect which steps the student is able to perform. A *paper-pencil* test may include a series of clock faces whose times are to be indicated. You might *ask* the child to reproduce time on a clock face and tell him or her to "think aloud," or you may simply observe the child's behavior as he or she sets a *real clock face*. Teacher-made diagnostic tests not only allow for a variety of response modes, but they also tap the mathematics in narrower bands than published tests. These narrower bands are amenable to analyses, and, therefore, gaps are avoided that are inherent in standardized published assessments.

The diagnosis for *addition of fractions with unlike denominators* might include the following test items. For the example $\frac{1}{3} + \frac{1}{2}$, a teacher-made diagnostic test might be comprised of tasks at the concrete and picture levels, as well as the following items in the paper-pencil mode:

1. Finding the lowest common multiple (LCM) of the denominators 2 and 3:

	1	2	3	4	5	6	7	8	9				
2	2	4	6	8	10	12							
3	3	6	9	12	15								

2. Solve open sentences:

$$3 \times \square = 6, \qquad 2 \times \square = 6$$

3. Rename the multiplicative identity:

$$1 = \frac{1}{1} = \frac{3}{3} = \frac{2}{2}$$

4. Recognize that the following notations are equivalent:

$$\frac{1}{3} \times \frac{2}{2} = \frac{1 \times 2}{3 \times 2}$$

5. Use multiplication of fraction algorithm:

$$\frac{1}{3} \times \frac{2}{2} = \frac{1 \times 2}{3 \times 2} = \frac{2}{6}$$

$$\frac{1}{2} \times \frac{3}{3} = \frac{1 \times 3}{2 \times 3} = \frac{3}{6}$$

$$\frac{2}{3} \times \frac{2}{2} = \frac{2 \times 2}{3 \times 2} = \frac{4}{6}$$

6. Use the addition of fractions concept when the denominators are the same number:

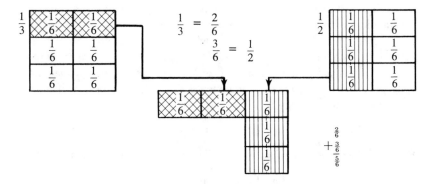

7. Move from the picture level in task 6 above to using the numerals and algorithms (symbolic level):

a. $\dfrac{1}{3} \times \dfrac{\square}{\square} = \dfrac{}{\text{LCM}}$

   $+ \dfrac{1}{2} \times \dfrac{}{\triangle} = \dfrac{}{\text{LCM}}$

b. $\dfrac{1}{3} \times \dfrac{\square}{\square} = \dfrac{}{6}$

   $+ \dfrac{1}{2} \times \dfrac{\triangle}{\triangle} = \dfrac{}{6}$

c. $\dfrac{1}{3} \times \dfrac{\square}{\boxed{2}} = \dfrac{}{6}$

   $+ \dfrac{1}{2} \times \dfrac{\triangle}{\triangle\!\!3} = \dfrac{}{6}$

d. $\dfrac{1 \times \boxed{2}}{3 \times \boxed{2}} = \dfrac{}{6}$

   $+ \dfrac{1 \times \triangle\!\!3}{2 \times \triangle\!\!3} = \dfrac{}{6}$

e. $\dfrac{1 \times 2}{3 \times 2} = \dfrac{2}{6}$

$+\dfrac{1 \times 3}{2 \times 3} = \dfrac{3}{6}$

_____

f. $\dfrac{2}{6}$

$+\dfrac{3}{6}$

_____

$\dfrac{5}{6}$

8. Transfer to addition of fractions with numerators greater than 1:

$$+ \begin{array}{l} \dfrac{2}{3} = \dfrac{2 \times 2}{3 \times 2} = \dfrac{4}{6} \\[2mm] \dfrac{3}{2} = \dfrac{3 \times 3}{2 \times 3} = \dfrac{9}{6} \end{array}$$

$$\dfrac{13}{6} = \dfrac{6}{6} + \dfrac{6}{6} + \dfrac{1}{6} = 2\dfrac{1}{6}$$

It is sometimes less threatening to the student if you put the test items on separate index cards. Then you can control the level of difficulty by presenting an easier task if the student seems anxious. It is important to remember that for those children who are overwhelmed by a page of mathematical tasks, one problem on a card may be less threatening. The experience of analyzing a concept into its mathematical components will organize your own thinking and enhance your teaching skills.

Guidelines for Preparing a Teacher-made Diagnostic Test

Following is a sequence of steps for building a teacher-made diagnostic test.

I. *Select content for your diagnostic test.*

List the areas of weakness for the class (or individual) that were identified on survey tests. (Survey tests include standardized achievement tests in arithmetic, end-of-chapter book tests, grade-level tests, exercises in the arithmetic text, or teacher-made surveys.)

II. *Isolate one concept that is to be diagnosed in depth.*

Apply the idea of requisite objectives (see Reisman, 1981) and learning sequences to analyze the components that make up the particular concept. Arrange these subconcepts in a logical teaching sequence so that prerequisite skills or concepts precede those behaviors that depend on them (see pp. 91–112).

III. *Determine at what level of learning the individual is (or at what level the majority of students are performing).*

A. Use Brownell and Hendrickson's (1950) or Gagne's (1965) hierarchies, described on pp. 92–106 of this book. (See also Reisman and Kauffman's (1980) hierarchy, p. 11.)
B. Administer Piagetian number conservation tasks, described on pp. 88–91, to determine if the student has such mathematical ideas as one-to-one correspondence, reversibility, identity, or seriation. These are basic to elementary school mathematics.
C. Apply Maslow's (1954) hierarchy of needs (see pp. 114–117 in this text) to determine whether the student's learning difficulties may stem from emotional or social needs rather than from intellectual causes.
   1. Observe the child in many school situations (classroom, playground, gym, lunch, free time).
   2. Make a home visit, if possible, to meet the child's family.
D. Decide where the student fits in Krathwohl, Bloom, and Masia's (1966) affective domain taxonomy (see pp. 117–120).

IV. *Decide on the behaviors you want the child to display in order to show what he or she has acquired the particular concept.*

Apply Bloom, Engelhart, Furst, Hill, and Krathwohl's cognitive domain taxonomy, as described on pp. 106–108 of this book.

V. *Write a table of specification that includes the behavior and content components to serve as the structure for your diagnostic test.*

An example of a table of specification found in the following chapter may serve as a structure for building a diagnostic test.

VI. *Build the test, asking the following questions:*
A. Is it all paper-pencil?
B. Will you need to include activities with concrete objects?
C. Will the testing situation parallel the teaching situation so that test items are a true reflection of the instruction?
D. Will you include extrapolation activities to show transfer of present knowledge to new situations?
E. Will you include items that require pointing responses for children who have difficulty producing a written response?

VII. *Interview the student (or class members) in regard to items missed in order to determine the validity of the item.*
Is the item really measuring what you think it is, or has the child missed it because of a misinterpretation of what is being asked?

Building a Diagnostic Test

The following activities provide a series of mini-tests, each built on a single concept or skill. You may build a file of single-concept diagnostic tests, and by combining these, develop broader tests. These examples of single-concept mini-tests are based on a task analysis of the main goal, entitled *Desired Behavior*.

Equivalent Sets

Desired Behavior: Recognize equivalent sets.

Requisite Objectives:
1. Recognize objects.
2. Name objects.
3. Match like objects.
4. Name like objects.
5. Identify like objects.
6. Pair like objects.
7. Pair unlike objects.
8. Match two sets of like objects in a one-to-one correspondence.
9. Select equivalent sets.
10. Perform behaviors 1 to 9 at the picture level.
11. Perform behaviors 1 to 9 at the symbolic level.

Table of Specification:

	Behavior				
Equivalent Sets	*A. Indicate*	*B. Name*	*C. Match*	*D. Identify*	*E. Pair*
1. Sets of objects					
2. Pictures of sets					
3. Sets of numerals or words					

Suggestions for diagnostic test items are keyed to the content and behavior as shown on the Table of Specification:

1A. Show child five red straws, five red blocks, and three yellow blocks. Say, "Point to the set of red blocks."

1B. For each set say, "Tell me what these are" (use objects in 1A).

1C.   Say, "Match the sets having red objects" (use objects in 1A).
1D.   Say, "Show me the set of three" (use objects in 1A).
1E.   Say, "Match the two sets having the same number of objects."
2A.   Show child drawing or pictures of objects. Say, "Point to the picture of red blocks."
2B–2E. Use the same procedure as that for sets of objects but use pictures.
3A–3E. Use the same procedures as 1A–1E but use numerals or words in place of objects.

Relations between Whole Numbers

Desired Behavior: Identify the larger (or smaller) of two numbers.

Requisite Objectives: 1. Count numbers aloud.
2. Enumerate objects.
3. Place sets in order of size from smallest to largest.
4. Assign a number to a set of objects.
5. Represent the ascending order of sets with numerals.
6. Identify the numeral representing the larger of two numbers.

Table of Specification:

	Behavior				
Whole Numbers	*A. Count*	*B. Enumerate*	*C. Assign*	*D. Represent order*	*E. Identify*
1. Numbers					
2. Sets					
3. Numeral					

Suggestions for diagnostic test items:

1A. Ask child to count aloud as far as he or she can.
1B. Ask child to enumerate objects in a set [Note the difference between counting and enumerating. Counting involves verbal associations (Gagne's Type 4 learning)]. Basic to enumerating is the notion of one-to-one correspondence.
1C. Show sets of objects. Ask the child to tell you how many objects are in a set.

1D. Place sets in order, smallest to largest. Tell the child to write numerals to represent the order of these sets.

2B. Show child sets of objects. Say, "Count the objects in this set." Continue with other sets.

2C. Say, "Write the numeral that shows how many objects are in the set."

3C. Same as 2C.

3D. Show sets having cardinal number properties of 1 to 9. Say same as for 2C.

3E. Show "7 to 9." Say, "Draw a circle around the numeral representing the larger number."

Place Value*

Desired Behavior: Write numbers named by two digits.

Requisite Objectives: 1. Select equivalent sets.
                              2. Identify the larger (or smaller) of two numbers.
                              3. Add whole numbers.
                              4. Multiply whole numbers.

Table of Specification:

				Behavior			
Place Value	*A. Select*	*B. Identify*	*C. Group*	*D. Name*	*E. Show*	*F. Count*	*G. Write*
1. Equivalent sets	✓						
2. Unequal numbers		✓					
3. Concrete objects			✓				
4. Number names				✓			
5. Number of groups				✓			
6. Objects in many-to-one relation					✓		

---

*See *Teaching Mathematics to Children with Special Needs* (Reisman & Kauffman, 1980) for information on teaching place value.

Table of Specification (cont.)

Place Value	Behavior						
	A. Select	B. Identify	C. Group	D. Name	E. Show	F. Count	G. Write
7. From 1 to 9 objects						✓	
8. Place values				✓			
9. Using place value						✓	
10. Abacus representation of 2-digit numeral					✓		✓
11. Picture representation of 2-digit numeral							✓
12. 2-digit numerals				✓			✓
13. Face value and place value of a digit in a numeral				✓			

Suggestions for diagnostic test items:

3C. Ask the child to bundle a collection of sticks into groups of 10 with from zero to nine extra single sticks.

4D. Ask the child to read aloud number names from zero to nine. Then following concrete level activities that emerge from prerequisite behaviors 9–13, extend reading aloud numerals beyond nine.

6E. Ask the student to show that a bundle of ten sticks may be represented by an agreed upon single object.

7F. Instruct the student to count from one to nine beads on a nine-bead abacus.

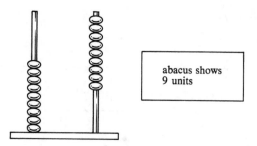

abacus shows
9 units

8D. Ask the child to name the place values of an abacus.

9F. Have the student count to ten on a 9-bead abacus by applying place value.

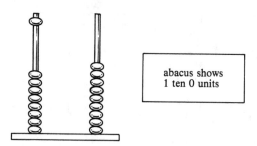

abacus shows
1 ten 0 units

10E. Say a number greater than nine and ask the child to show this number on the abacus.

10G. Show a two-digit number on the abacus and tell the child to write the number shown.

11G. Ask the child to write two-digit numerals from picture representations.

12G. Ask the child to write the numerals from 19 through 30. (This activity may be extended from 10 to 99).

12D. Ask the child to read aloud the numerals from 19 through 30. (Extend from 10 to 99).

13D. Ask the child to state the face value and place value of a digit in a numeral.

Extension of 12D. Ask child to read aloud:

45   378   9867   303

Extension of 12B. Ask the child to write an X on the correct numeral as you read aloud from the following table:

7	7831	1500	436
403	6	909	90
391	43	330	8

Extension of 12G. Dictate the following for the child to write as a numeral:

1. thirty-five   2. one hundred three

3. nine thousand four hundred twenty

Addition of Whole Numbers with Renaming

Desired Behavior: Add, with renaming, a one-digit number to a two-digit number.

Requisite Objectives: 1. Compute correctly the basic addition combinations.
2. Write a numeral correctly by employing place value.
3. Rename ten ones as one ten.
4. Compute using addition algorithm.

Table of Specification:

	Behavior		
Addition with Renaming	A. Compute	B. Write	C. Rename
1. Basic addition combinations			
2. Numeral			
3. Ones and tens			
4. Addition algorithm			

Suggestions for diagnostic test items:

1A. Ask the child to compute the basic addition combinations by completing the addition grid:

+	0	1	2	3	4	5	6	7	8	9
0										
1										
2										
3										
4										
5										
6										
7										
8										
9										

2B. Ask child to complete the following in the form:

3 ones, 2 tens = $\underline{23}$

1. 7 ones, 4 tens = _____
2. 3 hundreds, 5 tens, 2 ones = _____
3. 4 thousands, 2 tens = _____
4. 2 ones, 3 tens, 9 hundreds = _____

2C. Ask child to complete:

1. thirteen ones = _____ ten, _____ ones
2. twenty-three ones = _____ tens, _____ ones
3. one hundred thirty = _____ tens
4. 347 = 2 hundreds, _____ tens, 7 ones

3C. Complete the following:

1. 3 tens and 4 ones = 2 tens and _____ ones
2. 17 ones and 9 tens = _____ tens and 7 ones
3. 2 tens and 75 ones = _____ tens and 5 ones
4. 9 tens and 83 ones = _____ hundreds, and _____ tens, 3 ones

4A. Compute:

1.	18	2.	75	3.	92	4.	84
	+ 9		+ 5		+ 8		+ 9

The next chapter presents a model for developing teacher-made mathematics tests. The goals upon which the sample tests were constructed for four clusters of grade levels are keyed to specific test items. Tasks at the concrete level are also included in instructional goals.

5

Reisman Sequential Assessment Mathematics Inventory (SAMI)

The Reisman Sequential Assessment Mathematics Inventory (SAMI) is a model for a teacher-made diagnostic screening instrument. The SAMI presented here* is comprised of four parts: Part 1 for kindergarten and grades one and two; Part 2 for grades three and four; Part 3 for grades five and six; and Part 4 for grades seven and eight. SAMI is also appropriate at higher grade levels for older students who lack basic mathematics knowledge. It may be necessary in some cases to administer a lower level part of the SAMI to those students who cannot perform successfully on even the initial items comprising the part of the assessment that is equivalent to their grade in school.

All items on this diagnostic tool are keyed to 18 mathematics ideas. This is to help you quickly identify those areas which are problematic to a student or group of students. Also presented are selected answers to items on the SAMI. Once the areas of weakness have been identified, specific performance objectives for instruction may be developed. The areas of strength aid in selecting instructional procedures that have proven effective with the particular student(s). In addition to analyzing results of the SAMI, it must be remembered that day-to-day observations are important. The student's emotional state must be considered as well as his or her cognitive activities.

Specific instructional goals (see pp. 66–71) were used as the structure for diagnostic items on the SAMI. These goals may also be used for developing instructional activities that form the instructional component of the Diagnostic Teaching Cycle.

The SAMI items are categorized as to their psychological nature (see Reisman & Kauffman, 1980, p. 11) and mode of representing curriculum or content for each item (see Appendix C). Preceding this categorization is the Table of Specification that underlies the Sequential Assessment Mathematics Inventory, Parts 1, 2, 3, and 4. Individual and class profiles are presented following the type of learning summary (see Appendices D and E for profile formats).

Instructional Goals Underlying the SAMI

Part 1: Grades K, 1, and 2

Content	*Goal*
1. Proximity	a. Place an object close to a given object
	b. Draw a figure close to a given figure.
2. Spatial Relations	a. Complete a puzzle.
	b. Move an object upward in space (down).
	c. Place an object under (over) a given object.

---

*This was the forerunner of SAMI referred to under *Published Assessment Tests* on p. 42.

Content	*Goal*
	d. Place an object within a given enclosure.
	e. Place objects in an indicated order.
	f. Place an object between two given objects.
3. Size	a. Select the larger (smaller) of two objects.
	b. Arrange objects from shortest to longest.
4. Numeration	a. Write the digits 0 to 9.
	b. Indicate the cardinal number property of a set by selecting the appropriate flannel board numerals.
	c. Write the numeral that represents the cardinality of a set.
5. Cardinality	a. Match objects in sets showing one-to-one correspondence.
	b. Enumerate objects in a set.
6. Classification	a. Describe what is alike about two or more objects (or sets).
	b. Arrange objects into groups so that all objects within a group are alike in some way.
7. Equivalent Sets	a. Label equivalent sets with the numeral that indicates their equivalence.
	b. Draw a set that is equivalent to a given set.
	c. Use the = symbol when appropriate.
8. Nonequivalence	a. Select the nonequivalent set from a group of sets.
	b. Draw a set that has a greater number of objects than a given set.
	c. Use correctly the inequality symbols ($<$, $>$).
9. Addition	a. Draw a number line to show a given addition sentence.
	b. Record an addition example shown by combined sets.
	c. Show the commutative property with objects, pictures, and/or addition equations.

Content	*Goal*
	d. Show the associative property with objects, pictures, and/or equations.
	e. Show the additive identity with objects, pictures, and/or equations.
	f. Add on an abacus.
	g. Compute without renaming.
10. Multiplication	a. Show union of disjoint equivalent sets as a model for simple multiplication examples.
	b. Record simple multiplication examples shown with objects and/or pictures.
	c. Relate the place value idea to multiplication.
11. Place Value	a. Show ten units as one ten.
	b. Show ten tens as one hundred.
	c. Describe why $9+1$ may not be expressed as a one-digit numeral in base 10.
	d. Compare our place value notational system with an ancient nonpositional system.
	e. Relate multiplication to generating place values.
	f. Enumerate beads on a nine-bead abacus showing that the $9+1$ sum is shown by a move to the tens position.
	g. Employ place value in addition and multiplication computations when recording the vertical algorithms.
12. Subtraction	a. Employ place value in subtraction when recording the vertical algorithm.
	b. Record simple subtraction examples shown with objects and/or pictures (no renaming).

Part 2: Grades 3 and 4*

Prerequisite: Ability to perform Part 1 of SAMI.

Content	*Goal*
12. Subtraction	c. Show subtraction as the inverse relation to addition.

---

*Part 2, Grades 3 and 4, also includes Objectives 6 through 12b.

Content	Goal

Content   *Goal*

d. Record the subtraction problem for simple verbal problems (no renaming).
e. Complete an addition-subtraction grid.
f. Subtract on a nine-bead abacus (no renaming).
g. Relate renaming one ten as ten units to the addition operation where ten units are renamed as one ten.
h. Subtract with renaming.

9. Addition of Whole Numbers

h. Add with renaming using objects, pictures, and/or algorithms.
i. Record the addition problem for related verbal problems, with and without renaming.

10. Multiplication

d. Write multiplication equations that describe sets and/or pictures.
e. Record multiplication equations shown on number lines.
f. Write the factors for a number.
g. Show the Distributive Property of Multiplication over Addition with pictures and/or equations.

13. Division

a. Show division on a number line.
b. Show uneven and even division with dot arrays.
c. Relate division as the inverse operation of multiplication.
d. Show division as repeated subtraction of the same number.
e. Compute simple division problems.

14. Prime Numbers

a. Write prime numbers.
b. Distinguish prime from composite numbers.
c. Write a composite number as a product of its primes.

10. Multiplication of Whole Numbers

h. Write the lowest common multiple (LCM) of two or more numbers.
i. Write the greatest common factor (GCF) of two or more numbers.

Content	*Goal*
15. Fractions	a. Divide a figure into a designated number of parts.
	b. Write the number of fractional parts into which a whole has been divided.
	c. Write the appropriate numerator to show how many parts of the whole figure is being considered.
	d. Write the appropriate numerator and denominator for a group of objects (either real or pictured).
	e. Write equivalent fraction names for the number one.
	f. Show fractions on a number line.
	g. Write equivalent fractions from concrete, and/or picture representations.
	h. Write equivalent fractions for a given fraction.
	i. Perform simple multiplication of fractions.

Part 3: Grades 5 and 6*

Prerequisite: Ability to perform Part 2 of SAMI.

Content	*Goal*
10. Multiplication of Whole Numbers	j. Complete a multiplication grid.
15. Fractions	j. Multiply mixed fractions.
	k. Divide fractions.
	l. Add fractions with like and unlike denominators.
	m. Subtract fractions with like and unlike denominators.
16. Decimals	a. Divide units by 10 to obtain decimal fractions.
	b. Add and subtract decimals with and without renaming.
	c. Multiply decimals.

---

*Part 3, Grades 5 and 6, also includes Objects 9c through 15i.

Content	*Goal*
	d. Divide decimals.
	e. Convert fractions to their equivalent decimal form.
	f. Convert decimals to their equivalent fraction form.
	g. Relate percent to decimal fractions.
	h. Solve percent problems.
17. Geometry	a. Find the supplement and complement of angles.
	b. Graph designated points on an *x, y* axis.
	c. Use metric measures.
	d. Find the perimeter of a given figure.

Part 4: Grades 7 and 8*

Prerequisite: Ability to perform Part 3 of SAMI.

Content	*Goal*
17. Geometry	e. Find the volume of a given figure.
	f. Find the diameter of a circle when the radius is given.
	g. Find the circumference of a circle when the radius is given.
	h. Find the area of a given figure.
	i. Draw a simple closed curve.
	j. Show translations and rotations.
	k. Identify figures that have line symmetry.
18. Probability and Statistics	a. Write as a fraction the probability of a given event to occur.
	b. Interpret bar graphs.
	c. Interpret descriptive statistics.

Directions for Administering the SAMI

Read instructions to the student when necessary unless the item is testing reading comprehension, as in verbal problem solving. For young children or for those who have had little success in mathematics, you may wish to copy the test items on index cards and administer only one item at a time. This

---

*Part 4, Grades 7 and 8, also includes Objectives 13a through 17d.

procedure will help to eliminate the possibility of the child's becoming over-whelmed at the sight of a long-looking test. Proceed from the lowest level of learning to the highest so that the student will experience success as he or she works his or her way up to the higher levels of learning. The index cards may be laminated for continued use. Feel free to modify test items to ensure that the students understand the language and intent of tasks.

Scoring of the SAMI

In scoring items on the Sequential Assessment Mathematics Inventory, an item is counted correct only if all of its components are answered correctly. This helps to compensate for a child obtaining parts of an item correct by chance or by guessing. (See Appendix A for selected answers.)

If the student answers 80 percent of the questions in one part of the inventory correctly, go on to the next part. If the student does not reach the 80 percent criterion, go back to the next lower grade level test (e.g., go from Part 2 to Part 1) in order to identify the level at which he or she is performing.

SAMI Part 1: Grades K–2

4a. Fill in the missing numbers. 0 __ __ 3 __ 5 __ __ 9	7b. Draw the same number of circles in Set B as are in Set A. Set A Set B
4c. Write the number to show that four objects are in the set. ____	7c. Write the equal sign in the box where needed. 3 □ 3 5 □ 7 9 □ 6 12 □ 12
7a. Write the correct number that shows how many are in each set. ____ ____	8a. Mark X on the set that has a different number from the others.

8b. Draw a set that is greater in number than this set.

8c. Write the correct sign in the box to make a true sentence.

6 ☐ 9   4 ☐ 2
3 ☐ 5   8 ☐ 9

9a. Show that $2+3=5$ on the number line.

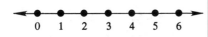

0 1 2 3 4 5 6

9b. Write the addition sentence.

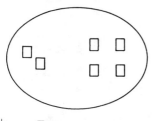

___ + ___ = ___

9c. Complete the following to make the sentences true.

$2+3 =$ _____ $+2$

☐ + ⊞ = ⊞ + ___

9d. Complete the following to make the sentences true.

$(2+3)+4 = 2+(3+$_$)$
$(\_+6)+7 = 8\ (\_+7)$

9e. Complete the following.

$3 +$__$= 3$

9g. Add the following.

41	24	17
+ 23	+ 13	+ 62

10a. Using the bags of candy, fill in the numbers below to tell how many pieces of candy there are.

___ + ___ + ___ = 6

3 twos = 6

$3 \times$ ___ = ___

10b. Write the multiplication sentence for this picture.

10c. Complete the following place value chart.

1000   ____   10   1

11a. Show how many tens by circling groups of ten.

11b. What number is ten groups of ten?
Write the number in the box below.

```
# # # # # # # # #     @ @ @ @ @ @ @ @ @ @
¢¢¢¢¢¢¢¢¢¢            ★★★★★★★★★★
% % % % % % % % %     $$$$$$$$$$
□□□□□□□□□□            &&&&&&&&&&
% % % % % % % % %     □□□□□□□□□□
```

12a. The problem $65 - 23 = \square$
can be written as

$$
\begin{array}{r}
65 \\
-23 \\
\hline
42.
\end{array}
$$

In the box below, write the
following problem this way
and find the answer.

$$47 - 32 = \square$$

11f. Mark the abacus that shows $9 + 1$.

ten one   ten one   ten one   ten one

12b. Complete the subtraction
sentence that tells about
the picture.

⊠⊠⊠⊠○○

$6 - \underline{} = \underline{}$

11g. Complete the following.

$$
\begin{array}{r}
32 \\
\times 24 \\
\end{array}
\qquad
\begin{array}{r}
36 \\
\times 23 \\
\end{array}
$$

Note: Part 1, Grades K–2, should
also include items based upon
performance Objectives 1 through
3b, which are at the concrete
level rather than paper-pencil.

SAMI Part 2: Grades 3–4

12c. Complete the following.

$$4+7=\underline{\quad\quad}$$

$$\underline{\quad\quad}-7=4$$

$$\underline{\quad\quad}-4=7$$

9h. Complete the following.

37	59
+26	+74

12d. Mark the sentence that solves the problem. Sam has 5 marbles. Jan takes 3 marbles away. How many marbles does Sam have left?

$5+3=8$ $5-3=2$ $3+2=5$

9i. Larry had 13 rocks in a sack. On his way home from school, he picked up 9 more rocks. How many rocks does he now have?

_____

12e. Complete the table.

+/−	6	3	2
8	14		10
4	10	7	
		12	11

10d. Write the multiplication sentence for the picture.

□□□□□   □□□□□   □□□□□

_____

12h. Complete the following.

62	35
−48	−19

10e. Show that $3\times3=9$ on the number line.

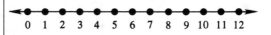

0 1 2 3 4 5 6 7 8 9 10 11 12

SAMI Part 2: Grades 3–4 cont.

10f. List factors for 18, greater than 1.

$18 =$ ____ $\times$ ____

$18 =$ ____ $\times$ ____ $\times$ ____

10g. Mark X on the correct number sentences.

$5(3 + 6) = 5(3) + 5(6)$
$5 + (3 \times 6) = (5 + 3) \times (5 \times 6)$
$5(3 \times 6) = 5(3) \times 5(6)$
$\square(* + @) = \square * + \square@$

13a. Show on a number line the number sentence $8 \div 2 = 4$.

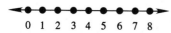

0 1 2 3 4 5 6 7 8

13b. Group the array to show
$17 \div 2 =$ ____

13c. Complete the following number sentences.

$18 \div 3 =$ ____

____ $\times 3 = 18$

13d. Show on a number line $15 \div 5 =$ ____ .

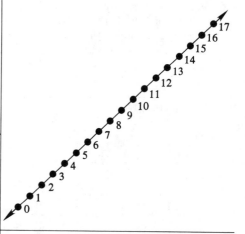

13e. Complete the following.

$8 \div 2 =$ ____
$6 \div 3 =$ ____ $3\overline{)15}$

14a. Write the prime numbers between 1 and 25.

___ ___ ___ ___ ___

___ ___ ___ ___

SAMI Part 2: Grades 3–4 cont.

14b. Circle the prime numbers.

1   6   2   8   11   18   22

14c. Write 24 as a product of primes.

24 = ___ × ___ × ___ × ___

10h. Write the lowest common multiple (LCM) of 8 and 6.

_____

10i. Write the greatest common factor (GCF) for 36 and 24.

_____

15a. Divide the figure into 4 equal size parts.

15b. Write the number to show how many parts the figure has been divided into.

15c. Complete the fraction to show how many parts are shaded.

_____

15d. Write a fraction to name the shaded part of the group below.

_____

15e. Write 3 fraction names for the number 1.

_____   _____   _____

SAMI Part 2: Grades 3–4 cont.

15f. On the number line below, mark
    X on the dot to show 5/6.

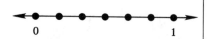

    0   1

Note: Part 2, Grades 3–4, should also include items based upon performance Objectives 6 through 12b.

15g. Mark X on the dot to show that
     1/2 = 2/4.

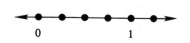

    0   1

15h. Write three equivalent fraction
     names for 1/2.

     1/2 = _____ = _____ = _____

15i. Complete the following.

       $2/3 \times 4/5 =$

       $7/8 \times 5/6 =$

SAMI Part 3: Grades 5–6

10j. Complete the following multiplication table.

×	5	7	3
4	20		12
8			
6			

15j. Complete the following.

$5\dfrac{1}{4}$
$\times 3$ 　　　　 $3\dfrac{1}{2} \times 2\dfrac{1}{4} =$

15k. Complete the following.

$\dfrac{7}{12} \div \dfrac{3}{4} =$

$\dfrac{35}{27} \div \dfrac{7}{3} =$

15l. Complete the following.

$\dfrac{3}{4}$ 　　　 $\dfrac{7}{8}$
$\dfrac{2}{+\,4}$ 　　 $\dfrac{2}{+\,3}$

15m. Complete the following.

$\dfrac{3}{3} - \dfrac{1}{3} =$ _____

$\dfrac{6}{8} - \dfrac{1}{8} =$ _____

16a. Write in decimal form.

$2 \div 10 =$ _____

$7 \div 100 =$ _____

16b. Complete the following.

$\begin{array}{r} 2.44 \\ +2.35 \end{array}$ 　　 $\begin{array}{r} 3.74 \\ +1.29 \end{array}$ 　　 $\begin{array}{r} 4.74 \\ -\ \ .35 \end{array}$

16c. Complete the following.

$\begin{array}{r} .23 \\ \times\ .2 \end{array}$ 　　 $\begin{array}{r} .43 \\ \times .12 \end{array}$ 　　 $\begin{array}{r} 7.3 \\ \times 2.4 \end{array}$

SAMI Part 3: Grades 5–6 cont.

16d. Divide the following decimals.

$.36 + .6 =$ _____

$.24 + .8 =$ _____

$.7 \overline{)48.3}$

16e. Write the following fractions as decimals.

$3/6 =$ _____ $5/10 =$ _____

$3/4 =$ _____ $2/3 \ =$ _____

16f. Write the decimals below as fractions.

$.23 =$ _____ $.25 =$ _____

$.3 =$ _____

16g. Write 75% as a decimal.

$75\% =$ _____

16h. Write 30% of 17.

$30\% \text{ of } 17 =$ _____

17a. Write the supplement of angle A.

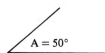

_____

17b. Graph the following points on the x,y axis below. (3,4), (2, −2), (−1,3).

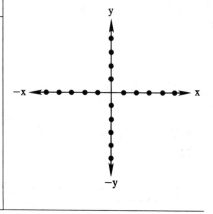

SAMI Part 3: Grades 5–6 cont.

17c. Complete the following.

6 cm = _____mm

3 km = _____m

17d. Find the perimeter of the given rectangular region.

3 cm

12 cm

Note: Part 3, Grades 5–6, should also include items based upon performance Objectives 9c through 15i.

SAMI Part 4: Grades 7–8

17e. Write the volume for the following figure in cm³.

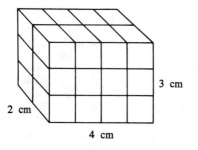

3 cm

2 cm

4 cm

_____

17f. Write the diameter for the given circle.

2 cm

_____

17g. Write the circumference for a circle whose radius is 6 cm.

17h. Write the area for the triangular region.

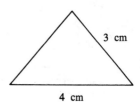

3 cm

4 cm

_____

17i. Draw a simple closed curve.

17j. Draw this figure in a clockwise 1/4 rotation.

_____

17k. Mark X on the figures that have line symmetry.

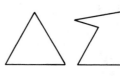

18a. Write the probability in fraction form for a coin tossed 10 times to come up heads.

_____

18b. On a visit to the zoo, Johnny saw bears, zebras, monkeys, and tigers. Write the number of bears and tigers he saw as shown on the graph below.

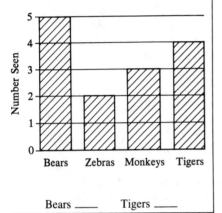

Note: Part 4, Grades 7–8, should also include items based upon performance Objectives 13a through 17d.

Bears ＿＿＿＿   Tigers ＿＿＿＿

18c. Following are test scores for 3 students, Ann, Barbara, and Catherine. Write who has the highest mean score. Write the highest mean score.

> Ann's scores: 89,72,80,56,98
> Barbara's score: 72,93,56
> Catherine's scores: 90,91,90,92,35

Student with highest mean is:

Mean = ＿＿＿＿＿

Individual SAMI Profile

Obtaining a diagnostic profile of an individual student's performance on the SAMI as shown in Appendix D, can give the teacher an "at-a-glance" picture of the student's strengths and weaknesses in areas tapped by SAMI. Items are arranged according to content areas as shown in Step 1. The teacher is to circle all items that were missed by the student. In Step 2, the number of correct items is found and then, in Step 3, translated into percentages of correct items within a content area. The graph under Step 4 allows the teacher to show the student's strengths and weaknesses on the test in the form of a profile by connecting dots placed in the graph that represent percentages.

Class SAMI Profile

The teacher may wish to know how the class as a whole achieved on each of the performance objectives that underlie the SAMI items. Appendix E includes a suggested summary sheet for showing the number of students who missed specific items. For each item on the test, count the number of students who missed item 1a under *Proximity, Spatial Relations, Size* and place a dot in the graph over this item. Do this for all items. If there are more than 20 students who took the test, add lines to the graph to accommodate 25, 30, 35, or more students. Then, connect the dots to form a class profile of items missed.

Applying the Diagnostic Teaching Cycle to Large Groups or the Entire Class

The use of individual profiles and class profiles is helpful in applying the Diagnostic Teaching Cycle to large groups as well as to an entire class. Teachers often inquire how to generalize diagnostic teaching to the whole class. They state that although the model appeals to them, it takes too much time in a real-life classroom. The diagnostic process is the same—whether working with one student or several. In applying diagnostic teaching to the whole class, the teacher should follow these steps:

1. Administer a screening test of some sort to either the whole class or to those students who are working on the same topics in mathematics. The screening test may be a standardized achievement test, a chapter test from a basal series, an end-of-the-book test, or a teacher-made test like the SAMI presented in this chapter. A published form of

SAMI (Reisman, in press) has been designed to include classroom diagnosis as well as short screenings and in-depth individual diagnosing. A kit for concrete assessments will also be available.

The purpose of this initial assessment is to identify broad strengths and weaknesses in one or more arithmetic topics by a number of students who have had similar learning experiences.

2. Group students according to their strengths and weaknesses as shown on the screening test. If students are in third grade or higher, show them how to complete their own profiles. Allow students to help each other in completing their individual profiles. The teacher will find that allowing peer cooperation is a good teaching strategy as well as a time-saver. Then arrange the individual profiles by content needs. For example, group all profiles showing a weakness in one particular arithmetic category. This procedure provides data for completing a class profile.

The class profile serves two purposes. First, it is a picture of class strengths and weakness in mathematics that provides direction for topics to be taught. The areas of weakness provide a second purpose. They should send up an alarm to the teacher to engage in some self-diagnosing of his or her teaching ability and techniques in the weak or low performance topics—especially if the same topics are consistently low across different classes. Thus, the hypothesizing component of the Diagnostic Teaching Cycle is initiated.

3. After screening, categorizing students' mathematics strengths and weaknesses, and deciding upon which students to group for instruction, the next step is to select instructional goals. See Reisman (1981) for an instructional scope and sequence chart based on task analyses of major topics that comprise the elementary school mathematics curriculum. Mini-lesson activities are also provided for major instructional goals.

4. The instructional phase of diagnostic teaching should focus on keeping as many students as possible on task for as long as possible. See Carroll (1963) and Harnischfeger and Wiley (1976) on the importance of time on task in relationship to achievement.

5. Formative evaluation occurs when teaching diagnostically, as corrective feedback is continuous. You obtain constant information on the daily status of your mathematics class, and you don't move on until students demonstrate an understanding of requisite objectives as well as correctly perform end goals. Thus, gaps in learning are minimized. Summative evaluation is also involved in the form of end-of-units tests. The important thing to remember is that it is the teacher who does the diagnosing—not the tests. The tests are tools for assessment,

but it is the teacher who interprets, analyzes, and utilizes the test information.

In summary, focus on large group instruction can be incorporated into diagnostic teaching of elementary school mathematics. With evidence holding that the more students are engaged in learning, the more they learn, trends in instruction are changing. It is becoming evident that the term *individualized instruction* has been misapplied when one student sits in a classroom all day, interacting with mathematics booklets. Individualized instruction means diagnosing the best learning experience for a student and providing situations in which he or she can learn. Several students in a classroom will likely have needs so similar as to warrant learning together.

6

Some Other
Assessment Aids for
Diagnostic Teaching

The more evidence that is obtained for diagnosing learning difficulties, the better your chances for helping the child. Perhaps the learning difficulty stems from a lack of readiness. Maybe the task to be performed by the child is too difficult for his or her level of learning. Previous instruction may have been inappropriate. Evidence should be obtained in all of these areas: the child, the task, and the instruction. This chapter includes some ways of tapping these three areas.

The Child's Readiness: Piagetian Tasks

Piaget (1965) has provided activities for observing whether a child has acquired various concepts basic to understanding the meaning of numbers. Here are a few activities based upon Piaget's work.

One-to-One Correspondence

Place six raisins in a row: ○ ○ ○ ○ ○ ○. Say, "Can you make another row that has the same number of raisins in it as this one?"

Or, in another activity, place six paper cups before the child in a row. Say, "Pretend that you are giving a party. You have cups for your party, but you need a napkin for each cup. Take these napkins (hand child about fifteen napkins) and match each cup to a napkin." The child then is to match up a napkin for each cup and recognize that he or she does not need to use some of the napkins. Failure on these last two tasks implies a lack of the one-to-one correspondence, which is a necessary prerequisite to number work.

Conservation of Number—A

Sit across a table from a child. Place two rows of objects (raisins, clay balls, crunched up pieces of paper, pennies, etc.), with six objects in each row, between you and the child. Place the objects in each row equidistant from each other so that both rows are the same length. Say to the child, "Are there the same number of _____ (name the object) in both rows?"

Row A ○○○○○○
Row B ○○○○○○

If the child agrees that there are the same number in both rows, you may continue with the exercise. If he or she does not, stop here because the child already has shown a lack of readiness for number concepts.

Next, spread the row of six objects out so that one row is longer than the other, although the number of both rows remains the same. Say again "Are there the same number of _____ (name of the objects) in both rows?"

Row A OOOOOO
Row B O O O O O O

Be careful not to help or hinder the child in answering by using cue words. For example, *do not* say, "Are there the same number of _____ in both rows *now?*" The word *now* may indicate that a change in number has occurred. Also, *do not* say, "Are both rows the same?" The child may be thinking of the absolute meaning for the word *same* instead of the relative meaning. The absolute meaning implies equality (only one row would be involved), while it is the relative meaning that implies equivalence (two rows having the same number of objects).

You are interested in whether the child can focus on the equivalence of the two rows rather than on the length of the rows. Children under five years of age usually respond, "There are more in the stretched out row." They are being fooled by their perception.

Piaget would have said that they are nonconservers of number. They begin to be conservers at the middle or end of their fifth year, and by the end of their eighth year, most are able to do this task. Before a child can compare equivalent sets and tell which sets have a particular number of objects, he or she must be able to observe the number property of a set without being distracted by color of objects, size, or spatial arrangements.

Conservation of Number—B

Place two rows of objects between you and the child, with six objects in each row and both rows the same length. Repeat the above question, "Are there the same number of _____ in both rows?"

Row A: O O O O O O
Row B: O O O O O O

Next, add objects to Row B without changing the length of either row.

Row A: O O O O O O
Row B: OOOOOOOOOOO

You now have changed the density of Row B, while leaving the endpoints equidistant. Repeat the question "Are there the same number of _____ in both rows?"

Conservation of Number—C
(Discontinuous Quantity)

Show the child two paper cups, each containing fifteen marbles. (See Figure 6.) Ask the child, "Are there the same number of marbles in each cup?" If there is doubt, let the student count the marbles. Then pour the marbles from one cup into a shallow pan. Ask, "Are there the same number of marbles in the cup and the pan?"

If the child is able to identify the fact that the number of marbles does not change even though the spatial arrangement of one set of marbles is more spread out, then the child is said to be a conserver of number. He or she is looking at the number property of the set and is not fooled by perceptual changes.

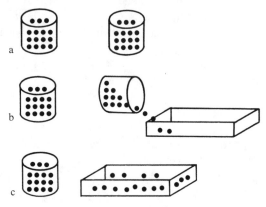

FIGURE 6 Conservation Task

Piaget (1965) also talks about reversibility* as a necessary component of conservation. By this, he means that the child is able to think, "There were the same number of marbles in both cups before the marbles in one cup were poured into the pan. If I were to pour the marbles from the pan back into the cup, I could see that the number of marbles in both cups would be the same again. So, since I can reverse the operation, the number of marbles does not change whether they are in the cup or in the pan." In his or her mind's eye, the child is able to reverse the appearance of the marbles in the pan to their previous appearance in the cup. This ability helps the child to ignore the change in appearance of the marbles; when he or she has developed this skill, attention will be on the number property and not the spatial arrangement of the marbles. This activity involves the concept of "identity." The set of marbles in the cup is the same set of marbles in the pan; therefore, the number property logically must be the same regardless of appearance. Success in this activity facilitates an understanding of addition, subtraction, multiplication, and division.

Serial Correspondence

Use straws of different lengths for this exercise. Say, "Can you make a staircase with these straws?" The child here is demonstrating a readiness for

---

*Operations are reversible, but thought is not (see Reisman & Kauffman, 1980, p. 104).

arranging objects in a specific order (from smallest to largest or from largest to smallest). Next, you might show the child sets of objects and ask him or her to arrange them in a certain order. For example, present sets of objects ranging in number from two to six. Say, "Which set has the smallest number of objects?" Guide the child to point to the set with two objects. Continue in this manner until all sets have been moved in a left-to-right alteration of smallest to largest, increasing by one object each time.

When the child is able to arrange sets of objects from smallest to largest with guidance, change your procedure to give the child less guidance. Give her five sets having from two to six objects and simply say, "Arrange these sets of objects in order from the smallest to the largest in number." You may vary your instructions by asking that the sets be arranged from largest to smallest in number. Also, you may present only even numbered (or odd numbered) sets and guide the child to arrange these in some order.

These activities provide a diagnostic profile of your student's readiness for number work. They are especially helpful in kindergarten, grades one, two, and three.

Children in kindergarten and grade one are developing one-to-one correspondence, many-to-one correspondence, conservation of number (the lasting equivalence of corresponding sets), seriation (ordering of sets), reversibility (ability to perceive mentally the original condition of a set of objects), and identity (the concept of "absolute sameness" where a set of objects is moved in either space or time; the set may undergo a change in location from a cup to a pan or it may be considered to exist both now and 10 minutes from now).

Usually by grades two or three, these relationships are demonstrable. If children in grade two or three are not able to perform these conservation activities, they may need quantitative experiences at the concrete level as prerequisites to performing mathematical computations at the symbolic level. Failure to perform these conservation tasks at these ages may also be indicative of a slower rate of cognitive development.

The Meaning of the Task

The teacher must be able to identify the specific desired learning and the conditions necessary for this type of learning to occur. Brownell and Hendrickson (1950) have presented a model that helps to determine the kind of learning involved in a particular learning task. They place learning products on a continuum of meaning.

(zero)   0 . . . ———— . . . N (maximum)

Knowledge that has a minimum of meaningful value would fall toward the zero end of the scale. For example, the numeral 2 is a label just as is the word *two* and has no rational explanation; it was selected arbitrarily. The letter *d* follows *c* and precedes *e;* once again; there is a minimum of meaning. However, the addition fact "2 + 2 = 4" moves toward the *N* part of the continuum. Involved here is the idea of "twoness," of "fourness," an understanding of equivalence (=), and an understanding of addition (+). Although 2 + 2 = 4 often is referred to as an addition "fact," it is instead a relational combination of concepts that Brownell and Hendrickson label *generalizations*.

Brownell and Hendrickson (1950) discuss four types of learning in their model: arbitrary associations, concepts, generalizations or principles, and problem solving. [Reisman and Kauffman (1980) describe a developmental mathematics curriculum based upon the psychological nature of mathematics topics.]

Arbitrary associations. These are facts that have no meaning. For instance, the fact that the numeral 2 stands for the number *two* is a human-made agreement that aids communication. When you see the numeral 2, you know it represents this many: xx. Another example is the word *table*, which stands

for the physical model of a table  . Success in learning arbitrary

associations is usually measured by the correctness and the quickness of the response.

Concepts. These are abstractions and must be taught through appropriate experiences with consideration given to the learner's background, interests, attitudes dealing with errors, motivation, and learning activities that he has already experienced. In discussing the retention of a learned concept, Brownell and Hendrickson suggest the importance of encouraging the student to put the concept to use. In such cases, the method of instruction may have been effective, but the infrequent use of the concept may be the diagnosed reason for difficulty in learning.

In learning basic mathematical concepts, it is important for the child to have motor experiences. Just as one cannot really get the idea of "hammer" without using a hammer, a child needs to manipulate sets of objects to abstract the number property of the set.

As an exercise, present a child with two sets of five objects and guide him or her to match these sets to one another on a one-to-one basis. First, give the child two sets having the same type objects (red blocks, yellow circles, white straws, etc.) and direct that he or she tell you what is the same about both sets. The child may say that both sets have "blocks," that they both contain "red blocks," that the blocks are "made of wood," or that both sets can be matched one-for-one.

Next, present a set of five red plastic straws. Say, "Now tell me what is the same about these three sets?" The child may say all three have "red things" and each set has five objects.

Then present a set of five yellow paper circles. Notice that the straws are plastic so that the only attribute that is now the same for all four sets is the number property: "fiveness." Ask the child to tell you what is the same about all four sets. He or she should say, "They all have five objects."

This sequence of experiences allows the child to attend to similar attributes: color, shape, size, and—finally—number. It is a process whereby the number concept is abstracted. The child now has a grasp of what "fiveness" means. He or she has actively used the senses of sight, touch, smell, hearing, and—perhaps—even taste to determine what was the same about the sets of five.

This abstraction process involves the child's ability to classify. If you wish to determine whether or not the child can classify, you might use the activity with the four sets just described and observe the child's answers. If the child is able to tell you what is the same about the sets, he or she is showing the ability to classify.

An alternate procedure for diagnosing a child's ability to abstract the number concept of sets involves a motor response. Instead of requiring a verbal response telling you what is the same about two or more sets, have the child do the following:

1. Show a set of five red blocks. Then give the child a set of six red blocks and say, "You make a set that is the same as the set I made." If the child uses all of the red blocks, he or she is not attending to the number property. Tell the child you see something that is not the same about both sets. Say, "Can you change something in your set to make it more like mine?" The child must see that he or she has one too many blocks before proceeding to Step 2.

2. Now bring forth a set of five red plastic straws and move your set of five red blocks away from the child's set of blocks and the set of straws, but still keep all three sets in the child's view. Say, "If you know something the same about your set (the five red blocks) and the straws, then move your set closer to the straws." The child may be responding to either color or number (if he or she matches only five blocks to the five straws) at this level. You need to present one more set to focus on just the number concept.

3. Move the set of straws aside and display a set of five yellow paper circles. Say, "If you know something about your set (child needed to

select only the five red blocks by now or should have stopped at Step 2) that is the same as this set (circles), then move your set closer to the new set.'' At this point, you have eliminated the attributes of shape, color, material, size, and function of object; only the common number property remains.

4. In Steps 1–3, there has been no need for verbal communication. As a diagnostic check, you now might say, ''What is the *one thing* that is the same about all of these sets?'' The child should say, ''They all have the same number of objects.''

When the child is able to abstract the number properties of sets, he or she is able to form relationships between two numbers. For example, the child discovers that ''threeness plus fiveness'' are ''eightness.'' He or she has formed a relationship between two concepts and that is known as a *generalization*.

Generalizations. These state relationships between or among two or more concepts. For example: $3 + 5 = 8$ is a generalization because the concepts three and five are combined by the addition relation. Generalizations are tools for problem solving.

Problem solving. This type of learning is initiated by a problem. Its success depends on a firm background of arbitrary associations, concepts, and generalizations. For example, in verbal problem solving in mathematics, the child needs to be able to perform the addition relation on the number concepts in order to solve the problem, ''Mary has three red pencils and five blue pencils; how many pencils does she have altogether?'' Of course problem solving is much broader than verbal problems [see Reisman and Kauffman's *Teaching Mathematics to Children with Special Needs* (1980) for creative problem-solving activities].

Implications for Instruction

Brownell and Hendrickson (1950) suggest that when you can identify whether your student is learning an arbitrary association, a concept, a generalization, or is problem solving, you are better able to decide what method of instruction to use.

Basically, there are two methods of instruction: the teacher tells (didactic method) or the student discovers (guided discovery method).

Arbitrary associations cannot be discovered. They are human-made agreements and must be transmittted by ''telling.'' However, concepts and generalizations lend themselves well to guided discovery teaching (the abstracting of the number *five* described above was presented in a guided discovery manner).

Since problem solving embodies arbitrary associations, concepts, and generalizations, it involves some telling and some discovery. Thus, the teacher must diagnose what type of learning (arbitrary association, concept, or generalization) is involved and determine the conditions necessary for its being learned. The following are examples of mathematics curricula that have been categorized according to Brownell and Hendrickson's (1950) hierarchy of types of learning:

Example: $3 + 5 = \square$
Type of Learning: Generalization (Principle)

Example: Draw a circle around the sets with five objects.

x	xx	xx	xxx	xxx
x	xx	x	x	xx
x		xx	xx	

Type of Learning: Concept

Example: Write the numeral to show three objects are in the set.
x x
x   _____

Type of Learning: Arbitrary Association

Example: $7 \times 3 = 3 \times \square$
Type of Learning: Generalization (Principle)

Example: State the axiom underlying the following examples.
$$7 \times 3 = 3 \times 7 \quad \underline{\hspace{2cm}}$$
$$4 + 6 = 6 + 4 \quad \underline{\hspace{2cm}}$$
Type of Learning: Generalization or Principle Learning

Gagne's Hierarchy of Type of Learning*

Another tool for diagnosing the type of learning with which the student is involved has been proposed by Gagne (1965). Gagne discusses two conditions for learning: internal conditions and external conditions. By internal conditions, he means those capabilities already possessed by the learner. The internal conditions of learning include all behaviors and capabilities that the learner needs for successfully approaching some new level of learning. Learning conditions that are external to the learner include those situations that are

---

*Adapted and reprinted from *The Conditions of Learning,* 2nd edition by Robert M. Gagne. Copyright © 1965, 1970 by Holt, Rinehart and Winston, Inc. Adapted and reprinted by permission of Holt, Rinehart and Winston, Inc.

outside of him and over which he may not have direct control. It is the external conditions that include those behaviors and activities we call "instruction." Gagne has presented a hierarchy of eight types of learning. He believes that in order for a student to learn a particular learning type (say Type 4), he must perform the skills necessary for Type 3. This hierarchy uses Gagne's notion of "necessary prerequisites."

The first two of the eight types of learning are Signal Learning and Stimulus–Response Learning. They represent the most basic forms of learning and provide the base upon which other more complex forms of learning are built.

Type 1—Signal learning. Signal learning is synonymous with the "conditioned response" that involves a substitute stimulus accompanying a particular response. The classic example for this learning is Pavlov's experiment in which he substituted the sound of a bell for food powder, which was followed by the flow of saliva in a dog's mouth. The bell (conditioned stimulus) is sounded just before spraying food powder (unconditioned stimulus) into the dog's mouth. The food powder had originally been accompanied by the saliva response (unconditioned response). Then the bell and the food powder are presented in close sequence with the bell preceding a spray of food powder by about one-half second, and the dog salivates. Finally, the bell alone is sounded and the saliva is emitted as shown below:

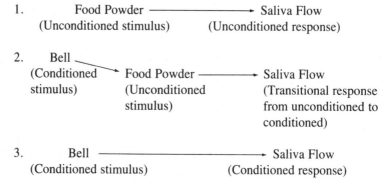

1.   Food Powder ——————————→ Saliva Flow
       (Unconditioned stimulus)   (Unconditioned response)

2.   Bell
       (Conditioned → Food Powder ——————→ Saliva Flow
       stimulus)   (Unconditioned   (Transitional response
                        stimulus)   from unconditioned to
                                              conditioned)

3.   Bell ——————————————————→ Saliva Flow
       (Conditioned stimulus)   (Conditioned response)

Step 2 is really a learning process. After the series of bell → food powder was repeated a few times, the signal or conditioned stimulus (bell) was accompanied by a learned response (the saliva flow) without the food powder.

Internal conditions for Type 1 learning involve natural reflexes, such as eye blink and salivation, and reflexive emotional responses including fear, anger, or pleasure on the part of the learner.

The two external conditions for signal learning are contiguity of stimuli and repetition. Contiguity in this sense means that both the signal and the unconditioned stimulus must be presented in close proximity to each other. The amount of repetition needed varies with the situation.

In applying this type of learning to teaching mathematics, consider the child's past experiences in learning mathematics. If success has been minimal or altogether lacking, a sick feeling may have been felt by the learner. In later grades, this same sick feeling may occur in response to the very request, "Take out your math books." Thus, it is important to investigate your student's past experiences in learning mathematics, for such investigation may throw light on present difficulties.

Type 2—Stimulus–Response learning. This differs from Type 1 in that the first type is concerned with reflexive responses over which the individual has little control. Type 2 learning emphasizes a single connection between some stimulus situation and some response situation. It is trial-and-error learning in which the first responses eventually are funneled to the desired outcome by rewarding only those responses that approximate the desired response.

The internal condition for Type 2 learning is the ability of the learner to make the learned response; the terminating response must provide satisfaction or reinforcement to the learner. The external conditions for Type 2 learning are contiguity and reinforcement. Withholding reinforcement results in the disappearance or extinction of the response.

An example of Type 2 learning may be a child's responding to flash cards. For example hold up $\frac{5}{+\,3}$ (stimulus); child responds "eight"; you smile, nod your head, and present another flash card (reinforcement). This does not necessarily imply that the child has any meaning for the stimulus. In fact, when flash cards are used prematurely in mathematics classes (that is, prior to the child's abstracting the number idea), the rote learning that occurs is Type 2 learning.

Another example of Type 2 learning involves the child's learning arbitrary associations. For instance, the child learns the names of numerals [1 ("one"), 2 ("two"), 6 ("six")] in a stimulus-response situation. The child is presented the numeral and responds with the numeral's name.

At a higher grade level, learning the names of the axioms exemplifies Type 2 learning. A student's learning the name *Commutative Property for Addition* may only approximate the correct response, but through repetition and reinforcement, the teacher finally guides him or her to the correct verbal response.

Type 3—Chaining. Chaining involves motor behavior. It implies that there is a series of motor acts in which the actions are connected one to the next. For the task to be successful, each individual S$\longrightarrow$R link must be performed correctly and in the right order. It is essential that the learner be able to perform the individual acts (e.g., opening a door).

The internal conditions of chaining involve the previous learning of each stimulus-response connection and the presence of kinesthetic feedback. The external conditions of Type 3 learning are getting the learner to sequence the links in a particular order, putting the links in close time succession (contiguity), repetition, and reinforcement. The first external condition, establishing the proper order of the links, may be accomplished in two ways. You may begin with the terminal link and work backwards, or you may start at the beginning and work toward the end of the chain with verbal prompting to guide the learner.

Examples of chaining are using scissors, catching balls, touch typing, buttoning, using a pencil, unlocking a door with a key, and starting an engine. So far as teaching mathematics, an example of chaining is a child's ability to write the numerals from 1 through 9 forming each correctly.

Type 4—Verbal association. This type of learning involves naming or labeling. Degree of meaning is not a part of verbal associations.

The internal conditions of Verbal Associations learning are the same as for Type 3. Each link in the association must have been learned previously as an S——>R connection. The external conditions include presenting the verbal units in proper sequence, actively involving the learner in the responding, providing confirmation of correct responses, and reinforcing these correct responses.

Examples of Type 4 learning are memorizing telephone numbers and poems, reciting the alphabet, and rote saying of multiplication tables.

Type 5—Multiple discrimination learning. This type of learning involves discrimination tasks such as distinguishing shape, color, texture, words, numerals.

The internal conditions for Type 5 learning consist of the learner's having acquired the four lower types. For example, if the learner is expected to discriminate between the numeral *3* and the capital letter *E,* he or she must have learned previously to associate the name verbally with its written character. The external conditions consist of prompting or cues, repetition, positive reinforcement, and the use of real or construction paper objects. In the beginning stages of the multiple discrimination task, the chains must be presented one at a time until the student knows them. Unless the learner knows the objects (or in some cases concepts) to be discriminated, he or she has no basis for comparing and selecting attributes for discrimination. Unless the child *knows* the numeral *3* and the capital letter *E,* he or she may not be expected to discriminate between them. Unless the child has already acquired the concepts "yellowness," "greenness," and "blueness," he or she will not be able to select objects similar in color to form sets as in the tasks which follow. Thus, it appears that there is a circularity to the hierarchy. Here is an instance when what appears to be a higher type learning is, at closer look, prerequisite to a lower type learning.

For a child to perform a discrimination task such as selecting a yellow object from assorted color objects, he or she must already have acquired the concept "yellow." How, otherwise, can a child hand you a yellow object? This may be considered an internal condition according to this theory. However, in diagnostic teaching, internal conditions may not be assumed. In fact, the identification of such a missing "internal condition" may well be the key to the remediation-instruction component of the diagnostic teaching cycle.

In applying Type 5 learning to teaching mathematics, we can use the example of set discrimination. Present a child with a group of objects, such as four yellow circles, two green squares, two blue squares, four green triangles, and four yellow straws (see Figure 7).

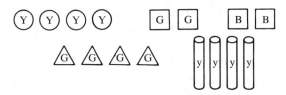

FIGURE 7   Discrimination Task

Now, present the child with tasks in regard to the following attributes:

Attribute 1–Color: Ask the child to make *three* sets with these objects so that all members of a set are the same color.

Response:

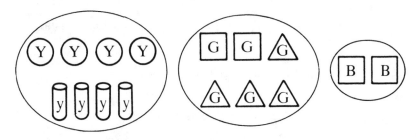

FIGURE 8   Discrimination Task—Color

Attribute 2–Shape: Say, "Make *four* sets so that all members of a set have the same shape."

Response:

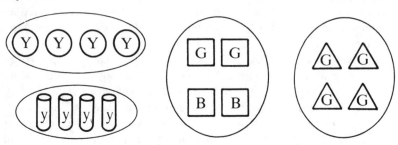

FIGURE 9   Discrimination Task—Shape

Attribute 3–Function: Given a pencil, a penny, and a block, say to the child, "Hand me the object you can write with."

Other examples of Type 5 learning are identifying different numerals, having the child select his or her coat from among others, or selecting a square blue object from other colors and shapes. This type of learning involves perception rather than conception.

Type 6—Concept Learning. Concept learning involves the meaningful labeling of a class of objects. The focus here is on abstracting similarities among objects in a set. The grouping of different sized circles and labeling them "circles" is an example of concept learning.

The internal conditions are the same as those established in Type 5 learning. External conditions include presenting stimulus objects simultaneously, cueing or prompting to aid the learner in identifying the common link in the stimulus situation, and reinforcement of correct responses.

Examples of concept learning include the fact that whales, dogs, cats are mammals, and understanding that the numerals *1, 2, 3, 7, 9* are symbols that represent numbers.

In mathematics teaching, the following are examples of testing for Type 6 learning:

1. Draw a circle around the even number.

   Response: 3   5 ⑥ 7   9

2. Draw a circle around the sets that show the number six.

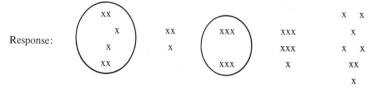

3. What number is represented in the place value chart?

tens	ones
	XX

Response: "two."

4. "Make *two* sets so that both sets have the same number of objects."

Response:

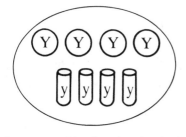
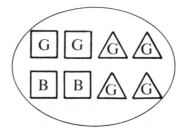

(or any combination showing 8 elements in a set)

FIGURE 10 Concept Learning—Cardinality

Type 7—Principle learning. A principle is a relational combination of two or more concepts. The internal condition is that the learner already knows the concepts which make up the principle. For example, in the principle *round things roll,* the concepts *round* and *things* must be within the learner's conceptual structure as does the meaning of the relationship *roll.*

The external conditions include the following:

1. Give the learner an explanation of the behavior expected. For example,
   "I want you to answer the question, what kinds of things roll?"
2. Question the learner so that he or she must recall the previously learned concepts.
   "Show me what things mean."
   "Pick out the round objects."
3. Use verbal statements that will lead the learner to put the principle together as a chain of concepts in the proper order.
   "Do all round things roll?"
4. By means of a question, ask the learner to demonstrate concrete instances of the principle.
   "Can you show me that all the round things roll?"
5. By the use of a suitable question, require the learner to make a verbal statement of the principle.
   "What kinds of things roll?"

Gagne presents evidence that the learning of high level principles is dependent upon the mastery of prerequisite low level principles. Examples of principles in teaching elementary school mathematics follow.

Commutative Property for Addition (CPA)
 For every two numbers, a and b:

$$a + b = b + a$$
$$3 + 8 = 8 + 3$$

Commutative Property for Multiplication (CPM)
 For every two numbers, a and b:

$$a \times b = b \times a$$
$$3 \times 8 = 8 \times 3$$

Associative Property for Addition (APA)
 For every three numbers, a, b, and c:

$$a + (b + c) = (a + b) + c$$
$$3 + (4 + 5) = (3 + 4) + 5$$

Associative Property for Multiplication (APM)
 For every three numbers a, b, and c:

$$a \times (b \times c) = (a \times b) \times c$$
$$3 \times (4 \times 5) = (3 \times 4) \times 5$$

Distributive Property for Multiplication over Addition (DPMA)
 For every three numbers a, b, and c:

$$a \times (b + c) = (a \times b) + (a \times c)$$
$$4 \times (5 + 6) = (4 \times 5) + (4 \times 6)$$

Additive Inverse
 A number added to its inverse sums to zero.

$$4 + (-4) = 0$$

Multiplicative Inverse
 A number multiplied by its inverse yields the number one.

$$\frac{2}{3} \times \frac{3}{2} = \frac{6}{6} = 1$$

Identity Principle for Addition
 For every number a:

$$a + 0 = a$$
$$87 + 0 = 87$$

Identity Principle for Multiplication
  For every number *a:*

$$a \times 1 = a$$
$$87 \times 1 = 87$$

Principle for Multiplying by 0
  For every number *a:*

$$a \times 0 = 0$$
$$87 \times 0 = 0$$

Type 8—Problem solving. The learner uses principles to succeed in a problem situation. As learning goes on, higher order principles emerge from the problem-solving situation. Problem solving involves four steps:

1. Presentation of the problem
2. Definition of the problem (This step distinguishes the essential features in a situation.)
3. Formulation of hypotheses.
4. Verification of hypotheses.

Conditions within the learner include the learner's ability to recall those principles learned previously that are relevant to his or her solving of the present problem. External conditions for Type 8 learning must provide for recall of the relevant principles so that these may be organized by the learner to achieve a solution. Verbal cues are provided to help guide the learner to the solution.

Examples of problem solving in teaching elementary school mathematics include verbal problem solving as well as discovery situations.

Example A: Mary has seven more dresses than her sister. If her sister has ten, how many dresses does Mary have?

Necessary prerequisites:

1. Learner reads the problem.
2. Learner analyzes verbal problem to select what information is given and what is wanted (Wilson, 1964).

Given	*Wanted*
Sister has ten dresses. Mary has seven more.	
	Number of dresses Mary has $= \square$

3. Learner translates verbal sentence into mathematical sentence.

$$10 \quad \triangle \quad 7 = \square$$

At this point, the child must decide on the appropriate mathematical operation (addition, multiplication, subtraction, division) to solve the problem. Guide the learner by asking about the wanted–given situation. If the wanted is a *whole* and the *parts* are given, then the operation will be either addition or multiplication. On the other hand, if the wanted is the unknown *part* and the given contains the *whole and known part,* then the appropriate operation is either subtraction or division. The meaning of the verbal problem is a clue for the learner to use in discriminating between which combining operation to use ($+$, $\times$) or between which separating operation to use ($-$, $\div$). The hardest part for the learner is deciding whether to use a combining or a separation operation. Once this decision is made, learners do not seem to have trouble deciding which operation within the combining or separating category to select.

In the example above, we are given the parts and want a whole. The obvious operation to use here is addition.

$$10 + 7 = \square$$

4. Finds solution. $\qquad 17 = \square$

Example B: Discovery problem-solving situation. Present child with paper circular region and a ruler. Ask child to find the length of the distance around the circle (circumference).

Necessary prerequisites:

1. Child can use a ruler properly.
2. Child's motor skills are developed to point where he or she can handle the circle, the ruler, and other objects such as string and pencils.

Solution 1: Child may obtain a piece of string, shoelace, or belt and place it around the circular region. Then child can measure the part of the string that went around the circle with a ruler. This is an indirect measure of the circle's circumference.

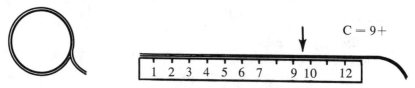

FIGURE 11 Indirect Measure of Circumference

Solution 2: Child may mark a point on edge of circle and roll it along ruler until point again touches ruler.

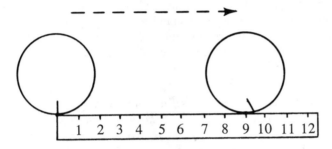

FIGURE 12 Measuring Circumference

Solution 3: Child may place the circle between two pencils. The distance between the two pencils then may be measured on the ruler. If the child knows the formula $C = \pi d$, he or she can find the measure of the circumference by plugging $\frac{22}{7}$ or 3.14 into the formula for "π," substituting the measure of the diameter for "d," and multiplying.

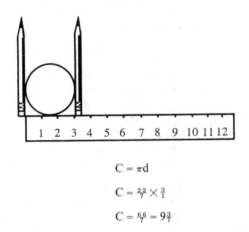

$$C = \pi d$$
$$C = \tfrac{22}{7} \times \tfrac{3}{1}$$
$$C = \tfrac{66}{7} = 9\tfrac{3}{7}$$

FIGURE 13 Formula for Finding Circumference

By using Gagne's (1965) hierarchy of eight types of learning and Brownell and Hendrickson's (1950) idea of the four levels of learning to identify the nature of the content to be taught, you can then decide upon the most appropriate method of instruction.

If you classify the content at the arbitrary association level in Brownell and Hendrickson's scheme, you know that there is a minimum of meaning imbedded in what is to be taught. However, principle and problem-solving learning are saturated with meaning. Figure 14 will help you visualize the connection between the level of learning and the more appropriate method of instruction. Notice how Gagne's hierarchy matches up with Brownell and Hendrickson's. Also, remember that this is a continuum that implies degrees of meaning and degrees of methodology rather than extremes.

Cognitive Domain Taxonomy

The final tool to be presented for use in dealing with intellectual aspects of diagnostic teaching is the *Taxonomy of Behavioral Objectives: Cognitive Domain* (Bloom et al., 1956). Included in this taxonomy are knowledge, comprehension, application, analysis, synthesis, and evaluation. These categories are useful tools for creating test questions or evaluative experiences for students of elementary school mathematics.

Knowledge involves recall of material stored in one's memory. It can be categorized as follows:

1.00 Knowledge

   1.10 Knowledge of Specifics

      1.11 Knowledge of Terminology
      1.12 Knowledge of Specific Facts

   1.20 Knowledge of Ways and Means of Dealing with Specifics

      1.21 Knowledge of Conventions
      1.22 Knowledge of Trends and Sequences
      1.23 Knowledge of Classifications and Categories
      1.24 Knowledge of Criteria
      1.25 Knowledge of Methodology

   1.30 Knowledge of the Universals and Abstractions in a Field

      1.31 Knowledge of Principles and Generalizations
      1.32 Knowledge of Theories and Structures

Comprehension comprises the individual's knowing what is being presented and using it without being able to tie the new learning to other learning. This category is classified on page 108.

Use of Didactic
or Telling
Method of
Instruction

↑
Use of Guided
Discovery
Method of
Instruction

Minimum
Meaning

Maximum
Meaning

Arbitrary
Associations

Concepts

Principles

Problem
Solving

Signal
Learning

Stimulus–
Response

Chaining

Verbal
Associations

Multiple
Discriminations

Concepts

Principles

Problem
Solving

FIGURE 14 Continuum of Meaning and Methodology*

*Adapted from "How Children Learn Information, Concepts and Generalizations," by W. H. Brownell and G. Hendrickson. In *The 49th Yearbook of the National Society for the Study of Education* (Chicago: University of Chicago Press, 1950). By permission of the National Society for the Study of Education.

2.00 Comprehension

    2.10 Translation
    2.20 Interpretation
    2.30 Extrapolation

Application is the use of learning in concrete situations.

3.00 Application

Analysis involves the breakdown of learning into its elements so that the relative sequence of these parts becomes apparent. This is similar to Gagne's concept of learning hierarchies. A further classification is:

4.00 Analysis

    4.10 Analysis of Elements
    4.20 Analysis of Relationships
    4.30 Analysis of Organizational Principles

Synthesis is putting parts together to form a whole that was not previously apparent:

5.00 Synthesis

    5.10 Production of a Unique Communication
    5.20 Production of a Plan or Proposed Set of Operations
    5.30 Derivation of a Set of Abstract Relations

Evaluation is making value judgments concerning such matters as the accuracy (see 6.10 below) of a situation or making judgments according to some criterion (see 6.20):

6.00 Evaluation

    6.10 Judgments in Terms of Internal Evidence
    6.20 Judgments in Terms of External Criteria

In order to present a model for using cognitive domain taxonomies, some exercises typical to elementary school mathematics are listed. Objectives are categorized according to Brownell and Hendrickson (1950), Gagne (1965), and Bloom (1956). Also included are Bruner's (1963) three modes of curriculum representation: enactive, iconic, and symbolic.

Activities for Elementary School Mathematics

Activity	Brownell & Hendrickson	Gagne	Bruner	Bloom
Identify number property of set	Concept	Concept	Enactive or Iconic	2.00 Comprehension
Identify cardinality of a set of objects	Concept	Concept	Enactive	3.00 Application
Identify sequences of counting numbers by ones, tens, and fives	Principle	Principle (also Verbal Association if little meaning to learner)	Symbolic	1.00 Knowledge 1.30 Knowledge of Universals and Abstractions in a Field
Write numerals 1–9 in sequence	Arbitrary Association	Chaining	Symbolic	1.00 Knowledge of Terminology
Associate numbers with points on a number line	Arbitrary Association	Multiple Discrimination	Iconic	2.00 Comprehension 2.10 Translation
Addition Using Associative Property	Principle	Principle	Symbolic	3.00 Application
Subtraction with Renaming (Borrowing)	Principle	Principle	Symbolic	3.00 Application
Multiplication using Distributive Property	Principle	Principle	Symbolic	3.00 Application
Multiplication using number line	Principle	Principle	Symbolic and Iconic	2.00 Comprehension 2.10 Translation

Activities for Elementary School Mathematics—Continued

Activity	Brownell & Hendrickson	Gagne	Bruner	Bloom
Division using separations of a set into equivalent subsets	Problem Solving	Problem Solving	Enactive or Iconic	4.10 Analysis of Elements
Write numerals shown on an abacus	Principle	Principle	Iconic and Symbolic	2.00 Comprehension 2.10 Translation
Use place value notation	Principle	Principle	Symbolic	3.00 Application
Multiply by 100	Principle	Principle	Symbolic	3.00 Application
Addition, no renaming, two-place	Principle	Principle	Symbolic	3.00 Application
Addition, renaming, three-place, zero in addends	Problem Solving	Problem Solving	Symbolic	3.00 Application
Column Addition, ragged columns	Problem Solving	Problem Solving	Symbolic	3.00 Application
Subtraction, renaming, zero in minuend (whole)	Problem Solving	Problem Solving	Symbolic	3.00 Application
Multiplication, no renaming, one-place by two- and three-place, zeros	Principle	Principle	Symbolic	3.00 Application
Division, no remainder, one- and two-place ÷ one-place	Principle	Principle	Symbolic	3.00 Application

Skill/Task				
Division, no remainder, one- and two-place ÷ one-place, zeros	Principle	Principle	Symbolic	3.00 Application
Division, remainder, one- and two place ÷ one-place	Principle	Principle	Symbolic	3.00 Application
Write sets of equivalent fractions	Principle	Principle	Symbolic	2.10 Comprehension, Translation
Classify objects to form sets	Concept	Multiple Discrimination, Concept	Enactive	4.30 Analysis of Organizational Principles
Counting aloud, one-to-one correspondence lacking	Arbitrary Association	Verbal Chaining	Symbolic	1.00 Knowledge
Enumeration, counting aloud—one-to-one correspondence present, example: counting objects in a set to find cardinality ("how-muchness" of set)	Concept	Concept	Enactive and Symbolic	3.00 Application
Solving verbal problems	Problem Solving	Problem Solving	Symbolic	5.00 Synthesis 5.20 Production of a plan, or proposed set of operations
Writing a number sentence from a word problem	Problem Solving	Problem Solving	Symbolic	2.00 Comprehension 2.10 Translation

By analyzing your mathematics objectives in this way, you can determine several things:

1. Are your test items covering the range of the taxonomy or are they all at the lowest level, 1.10 Knowledge of Specifics?
2. Are you evaluating only arbitrary associations or are you also including activities that tap the higher levels of learning?
3. Are your evaluations always at the symbolic level, or do you include enactive and iconic activities, too?
4. Are you aware of the necessary prerequisite learning implicit in an activity? This strategy for thinking will force you to identify these necessary prerequisites.
5. The use of these tools will help you to diagnose gaps in your students' mathematical foundations.
6. These tools will help you to decide what methods and materials are most appropriate for teaching various parts of your mathematics curriculum.

7

Diagnosing in the
Affective Domain

Emphasis usually is placed on teaching and testing in the cognitive domain, but if you take one look around an elementary school classroom, it soon becomes obvious that we also need to deal with the affective domain. I have seen children become completely disabled, both intellectually and emotionally, following a rebuff from the teacher. Many times the child had pushed the teacher beyond all limits knowing that he or she was asking for disciplinary measures, but when the discipline came, the child would react with surprise, anger, or complete withdrawal. According to Abraham Maslow (1962),

> the healthy child is able to be justifiably angry, self-protecting and self-affirming, i.e., reactive aggression. Presumably, then, a child should learn not only how to control his anger, but also how and when to express it. (p. 36)

Maslow has presented a hierarchy of needs that is an excellent diagnostic tool in dealing with children as well as adults. Use of this hierarchy helps to explain children's behavior and teachers' reactions to such behavior.

Maslow's Hierarchy of Needs*

Basic in Maslow's hierarchy are the level of physiological needs. Built upon the physiological needs—in order—are the safety needs, the need to love and to be loved, the self-esteem needs, and the self-actualization level. (See Figure 15.)

Physiological Needs

A child who is hungry, cold, ill, terrified, exhausted, or has to go to the bathroom will not be listening to your explanation of prime factors and their relation to multiplication. Such a child would be at Maslow's physiological needs level and probably would not even hear your words. This level is the most basic and must be satisfied before progress to the next level can occur.

Have you ever encountered a situation where you have been reduced to the physiological level? As is the case with all of these needs, it will be helpful if you place yourself on the hierarchy by remembering appropriate situations that you may have been in yourself. The better you understand the feelings one has at the various levels, the more empathy you will have for your students. Instead of taking observable behavior at face value, you will be in a position to diagnose *why* the child is exhibiting a particular behavior. For

---

*Based on *Motivation and Personality*, 2nd ed., Chapter 4, by Abraham H. Maslow. Copyright © 1954 by Harper & Row, Publishers, Inc. Copyright © 1970 by Abraham H. Maslow. By permission of Harper & Row, Publishers, Inc.

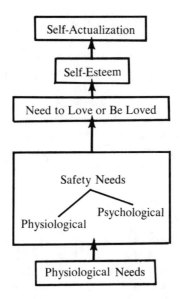

FIGURE 15   Maslow's Hierarchy of Needs

example, the underachiever often appears academically disabled in a cognitive sense when the trouble may really stem from the affective domain.

I have seen elementary school children fall sound asleep at their tables or desks amid the noise of a busy classroom. Teachers explained that they let particular children sleep because they had found that the home conditions were not conducive to the children's getting proper amounts of sleep. This is the real world, and teachers must be aware of such conditions if they are to reach children effectively. Many school districts have offered free or inexpensive breakfast programs for children. Federal budget restrictions may curtail these programs, making teachers' attention to physiological needs crucial.

Safety Needs

Maslow divided safety needs into two types—physical and psychological.

Physical safety. An example of a child's not being free to learn because the physical safety need has not been met is exemplified by the youngster who was threatened by a neighborhood gang. The threat "I'm gonna get you" can do much to prevent a child from learning in the classroom. A child in the classroom of a teacher who engages in physical punishment also may live in fear for his or her physical safety. Children who are physically abused at home are further examples of the physical safety level's not being met.

Psychological safety. Closely tied to the level of physical need is the psychological safety level. A child sitting in a classroom worrying about the fight his or her parents had that morning cannot concentrate on academic endeavors. If the child thinks the teacher does not like him or her, he or she is not psychologically safe and will have learning difficulties when interacting with this teacher. The first grader who is bussed across town to a strange school in a strange neighborhood will need to develop a feeling of safety before he or she can be expected to concentrate on academic learning. It is important that the teacher in the receiving school recognize those children who have not satisfied their psychological safety level and aid them in attaining a feeling of personal security.

The Need for Love and the Need to Be Loved

The next need on Maslow's hierarchy deals with love. Children must be able to love themselves before they can love others. Their self-concepts are very much tied up with this level. If children feel loved, they are free to engage in academic activities. They know that they will continue to be loved under all circumstances. The child whose parents make him or her buy love with high grades does not feel satisfied in this need. Many underachievers are performing poorly in school as a result of their need for love not being fulfilled.

The Need for Self-Esteem

This need involves status, recognition, and attention. The peer culture is important in satisfying the need for self-esteem. Many times the child who is not perceived by the teacher as having status in the classroom has a high degree of recognition from friends. It is important for the teacher to diagnose what activities receive status value among the peer groups. In the 1940s, it was considered "square" for a teenager—especially a girl—to obtain high grades in school. The 1960s began a marked change in peer values. In fact, in the area of mathematics, the 1957 Russian Sputnik space shot initiated the development of a high level of esteem for successful mathematics students in the United States that has continued into the eighties.

Self-esteem is a by-product of success. In order to insure that every mathematics student tastes some success, a diagnostic strategy for teaching mathematics is essential. The meshing of the student's cognitive level with the appropriate portion of the task to be learned will help to insure success for the mathematics student. When children taste success, they are also experiencing a measure of self-esteem. The teacher recognizes them with words of praise or good grades, and the children have a sense of well-being.

This need may be satisfied at very early ages in academic areas when a diagnostic strategy is employed. The gifted first grader may excel in mathematics class only if the curriculum is appropriate for his or her cognitive structure. For instance, there are bright first graders who cannot tell time to the minute. In fact, they may not even be exposed to this skill until third grade. However, when the skill is analyzed and a more appropriate sequence of instruction identified, success can be achieved by the first graders. A feeling of self-esteem is present every time these children are asked what time it is and they are able to respond correctly. They will smile and stand up very straight as they receive their praise.

Self-actualization

Maslow considered self-actualization as a "peak experience" occurring mainly in adults. However, I believe that elementary school children can encounter peak experiences. The first-grade children described above, who can correctly identify time to the minute, appear as though they may have been undergoing a fleeting self-actualizing experience.

When Maslow's hierarchy of needs is used as a tool for diagnosing emotional needs of both student and teacher, increased communication and understanding result. This hierarchy has a great deal of power when applied to parents in an attempt to help them understand their position in relation to their child, who is also your student. The hierarchy helps teachers to understand their emotional reactions to a student or class and aids them in selecting appropriate behavior when dealing with difficult situations.

Since Maslow's scheme is a hierarchy, prior needs must be satisfied in order to attain a higher level. However, an individual may be at different levels in various subject areas or parts of his or her other life at different times. For example, one minute a student may be at the self-esteem need as he or she discusses nondecimal numeration systems, and the next the child may be reduced to the psychological safety need as a loud clap of thunder or a nearby explosion occurs. An earthquake might lower the child to the physical safety need and a severe stomach cramp to the most basic need, the physiological level.

Taxonomy: Affective Domain*

The affective domain taxonomy helps structure your thinking in diagnosing the attitudes, interests, appreciations, and values of your students in regard to elementary school mathematics. At its lowest level, this taxonomy focuses on

---

*This section is based on *Taxonomy of Educational Objectives, Handbook 2: Affective Domain* by D. R. Krathwohl, B. S. Bloom, and B. B. Masia (New York: David McKay and Co., 1964). Used by permission.

the student's awareness of mathematics concepts (is he or she simply able to perceive them?). Next, it is concerned with a response to mathematics (is he or she doing something with mathematics?). The third step of the affective domain taxonomy involves values (does the student perceive mathematical endeavors as having worth?). At the fourth step, the student organizes values into some sort of a structure (he or she looks at the relationships among these values and some emerge as being more important than others). The highest level of this taxonomy, called *characterization,* involves organizing the inter-relationships among values into a philosophy of life. (It is at this level that a system of values, beliefs, ideas, and attitudes is created by the student).

Since attitudes and emotions seem to be directly involved in learning mathematics, a diagnostic strategy of teaching mathematics must include awareness of a student's affective domain.

The affective domain taxonomy will clarify levels of emotive behaviors and will help to categorize behavioral objectives dealing with attitudes toward mathematics and with learning this subject. Examples of how to make use of this taxonomy follow.

1.0 Receiving (Attending): Audiovisual devices are helpful in capturing the child's attention at this level, which has three components:

1.1 Awareness
1.2 Willingness to Receive
1.3 Controlled or Selected Attention

An example of Awareness (1.1) is the child who realizes the importance of identifying what he or she does not understand in arithmetic, listens more carefully (1.2), and pays particular attention when the teacher reviews a weak area (1.3).

Objectives here might include the development of awareness of the importance of early recognition and treatment of a problem in arithmetic, willingness to take part in review sessions, and preference for addition over subtraction.

2.0 Responding: This category goes beyond the mere intention of doing something; it involves some action. This level also has three parts:

2.1 Acquiescence in Responding
2.2 Willingness to Respond
2.3 Satisfaction in Response

In Acquiescence in Responding (2.1), the desired behavior is described as compliance to teacher demands. Objectives at this level are directed at safety rules or discipline. The Willingness to Respond level (2.2) involves voluntary action on the part of the student. The next level (2.3) implies a satisfaction on the learner's part.

Suggested objectives for the 2.0 categories include the completion of mathematics homework, voluntary reading about mini-computers, and a broad smile from the student upon solving a linear equation.

3.0 Valuing: This category involves the idea that mathematics has worth and that learning mathematics is a worthwhile endeavor. There are three parts to the valuing category:

3.1 Acceptance of a Value
3.2 Preference for a Value
3.3 Commitment

Acceptance of a Value (3.1) involves exhibiting behavior that shows a belief in the worth of the activity. Behavior at the Preference for a Value level (3.2) is a bridge between 3.1 and 3.3. It involves more than just accepting a value, but less than commitment. Commitment (3.3) involves loyalty and certainty. At this level, the student is motivated by an underlying tension that needs to be satisfied.

Suggested objectives are continued conversation about a mathematics concept by the student with friends outside of classroom situation, active participation in arranging a math and science fair, and indication of a long-term value for mathematics by the student.

4.0 Organization: Since some learning involves more than one value, it is necessary to organize values into a system, identify the relations between values, and notice the more powerful and lasting values. The two subsets of organization are:

4.1 Conceptualization of a Value
4.2 Organization of a Value System

The Conceptualization of a Value category (4.1) permits the student to see how the new value fits into his or her value system. The Organization of a Value System (4.2) consists of ordering one's concepts and makes allowances for the emergence of new values.

Suggested objectives here are the student's identification of the characteristics of a mathematical activity that he or she admires, and the student's development of a plan for regulating "math homework time" with "play time."

5.0 Characterization: At this level, the values are already in a hierarchy that has determined behavior. The two components of characterization are:

5.1 Generalized Set
5.2 Characterization

The Generalized Set level (5.1) may be considered a predictor or source of determination of the student's behavior. The Characterization category (5.2) defines the individual's philosophy of life. For example, the commitment to high academic achievement is shown by high level of performance in all academic areas.

Suggested objectives here are revision of the student's judgment in the light of new facts and demonstration of consistently high achievement behavior in all areas.

An Instrument for Tapping Attitudes

Now that you have a structure for diagnosing in the affective domain, you need a simple instrument for measuring attitudes toward mathematics. The semantic differential technique (Osgood, Suci, & Tannenbaum, 1957) is a helpful tool for use in tapping attitudes. It is made up a list of bipolar adjectives weighted on a seven-point scale. An example follows.

Addition

1.	UGLY	-3 -2 -1 0 1 2 3	BEAUTIFUL
2.	CHANGELESS	__ __ __ __ __ __ __	CHANGING
3.	WINDY	__ __ __ __ __ __ __	CALM
4.	STRANGE	__ __ __ __ __ __ __	FAMILIAR
5.	UNEXPLORED	__ __ __ __ __ __ __	EXPLORED
6.	UNPLEASANT	__ __ __ __ __ __ __	PLEASANT
7.	BAD	__ __ __ __ __ __ __	GOOD
8.	DIRTY	__ __ __ __ __ __ __	CLEAN
9.	HARMFUL	__ __ __ __ __ __ __	HELPFUL
10.	WORTHLESS	__ __ __ __ __ __ __	VALUABLE

The scale may be weighted in the following manner: -3 -2 -1 0 $+1$ $+2$ $+3.$ Write the name of the concept to be tapped at the top of the set of scales. Add the plus scores and subtract the sum of the minus scores for each concept tapped. Then find the mean score. A positive score indicates a positive attitude.

Some other examples of concepts that might be measured in this way are subtraction, division, multiplication, geometry, mathematics teachers, school, I-as-a-student, I-as-a-person.

Let us review the reactions of a student to the concept "I-as-a-person" and see how the attitude measure is derived.

I-as-a-Person

1.	UGLY	__ __ X__ __ __ __ __	BEAUTIFUL
2.	CHANGELESS	__ __ __ X__ __ __ __	CHANGING
3.	WINDY	__ __ X__ __ __ __ __	CALM
4.	STRANGE	__ __ __ __ X__ __ __	FAMILIAR
5.	UNEXPLORED	__ __ X__ __ __ __ __	EXPLORED
6.	UNPLEASANT	__ __ __ X__ __ __ __	PLEASANT
7.	BAD	__ __ __ X__ __ __ __	GOOD
8.	DIRTY	__ __ __ X__ __ __ __	CLEAN
9.	HARMFUL	__ __ __ X__ __ __ __	HELPFUL
10.	WORTHLESS	__ __ __ X__ __ __ __	VALUABLE

The numerical weightings for each bipolar pair are

1. -1	2. 0	4. $+1$
3. -1	6. 0	
5. -1	7. 0	
	8. 0	
	9. 0	
	10. 0	

$-3 + 0 + 1 = -2$. Then divide this sum of -2 by 10 (the number of bipolar pairs). Thus the score is $-.2$ for this concept.

A mean score of $-.2$ is obtained as the profile weighting for this child on the concept, "I-as-a-person." If other concepts show up negatively as well, you should apply Maslow's hierarchy of needs and Krathwohl, Bloom, and Masia's affective domain taxonomy rather than emphasizing only the cognitive domain.

This is an oversimplified modification of Osgood's semantic differential. However, for the classroom teacher's use, a comparison of many children's scores on this task with their mathematics performance will prove helpful in identifying attitudes of children toward arithmetic topics.

Concept of the Integrated Person*

Carl Rogers (1959) has suggested that the client-centered psychotherapeutic situation may be compared to the student-teacher relation. Significant learning occurs in the psychotherapeutic relationship in much the same way as in the student-teacher relationship. This learning is more than mere accumulation of facts. It makes a difference in the individual's behavior. The course of action the individual chooses in the future also is affected, as well as his or her attitude system and personality.

Rogers (1959a) presents five conditions of learning in psychotherapy. They are listed below.

1. Facing a problem
2. Congruence
3. Unconditional positive regard
4. Empathetic understanding
5. Perception of therapist's congruence

These are described below and applied to an educational setting.

Facing a Problem

The individual is faced with a problem which he or she has tried—unsuccessfully—to cope with. The individual is eager to learn how to handle the problem but, at the same time, may be frightened about making a disturbing discovery. Thus, one condition of learning is an uncertain and ambivalent desire, growing out of a perceived difficulty, to learn or to change.

The student who has met a challenge in mathematics performance is experiencing this uncertain and ambivalent desire to learn but also may be frightened that the cause is unpleasant. The student may be anxious to determine why he or she cannot divide decimal fractions, but may, at the same time, be resistant to help because he or she believes he or she is dumb.

Taking the comparison of the client-therapist relationship a step beyond the student-teacher situation, further comparisons may be made regarding teacher-principal, teacher-supervisor, and principal-superintendent interactions. Teachers whose children have shown up consistently low in mathematics achievement may well be ambivalent in their desire to identify reasons for the poor performance of the class. Refresher courses in mathematics content or in how children learn elementary school mathematics may be needed. Are

---

*This section is based on "Significant Learning: In Therapy and in Education," by Carl R. Rogers, *Educational Leadership*, 1959, *16*, 4. Reprinted by permission.

teachers working at a concrete level when necessary or is it too much trouble to get out the manipulative materials? Are they able to identify the causes of students' low performances as resulting from instruction or is it always the students' faults?

The principal whose entire school is performing poorly on mathematics achievement tests is facing a problem with his or her superintendent. Does the principal place the blame on the student population, on the teachers, on the atmosphere that he or she has created in his school building, or is he or she able to identify that the tests are not appropriate to the mathematics curriculum of the school? Is the principal able to seek help from superiors or colleagues? Is he or she able to face the problem, or even sure that it is a problem?

Congruence

Just as the therapist must be fully aware of what he or she is experiencing in the client-therapist relationship, so too must the teacher be aware of his or her own experiences. The teacher must be accepting of immediate feelings and make others feel comfortable and secure with him or her.

Unconditional Positive Regard

The quality of unconditioned positive regard is best exemplified by the expression "I care." Involved is a safety-creating climate and the acceptance of both positive and negative expressions. Students who know they can fail and still be accepted by those they love and respect will not feel that they must buy love with high achievement. When children know that they will not be rejected or punished for poor achievement, they will not feel the need to cheat on evaluations. The "I care" attitude of the diagnostic teacher comes across to the students, who then begin to care about themselves.

Empathetic Understanding

Empathetic understanding involves sensing the client's (or student's) world as if it were your own, without ever losing the "as if" quality. You sense the student's anger, fear, or confusion *as if* it were your own yet do not allow your own anger, fear, or confusion to get bound up in it. It is then that you can help make your student aware of feelings and guide him or her to understand them.

Often a student will become angry and not try to work out a mathematics problem. If you can empathize with the student's feelings without allowing yourself to become angry, you can better help to bring about a positive behavior in the student.

Perception of Therapist's Congruence

As the client must perceive and experience the therapist's congruence, acceptance, and empathy, so must the student. These conditions in the teacher must be communicated to the student.

When these five conditions exist, a process of change occurs. Students' rigid perceptions of themselves and others loosen and become open to reality. Rogers (1959a) has said that motivation doesn't come from the therapist (teacher) or the client (student), but, rather, "motivation for learning and change springs from the self-actualizing tendency of life itself, the tendency for the organism to flow into all the differentiated channels of potential development, insofar as these are experienced as enhancing" (p. 4).

Implications for Education

There are several implications for education imbedded in Rogers' (1959b) ideas. He seems to suggest "permitting the student at any level to be in real contact with the relevant problems of his existence so that he perceives those problems and issues which he wishes to resolve" (p. 186). The teacher's role, then, is to create a facilitating classroom climate in which real learning takes place. Then the teacher becomes a real person, not a "faceless embodiment of a curriculum requirement, or a sterile pipe through which knowledge is passed from one generation to the next" (p. 190).

The teacher must be aware that such accepting and empathetic behavior may free students to express attitudes about parents, hatred of siblings, and feelings of concern about themselves as they meet new situations and new material. Do such feelings have a right to exist openly in a school setting? Rogers says, "Yes. They are related to a person's becoming, to his effective learning and functioning" (p. 253).

Dealing with these feelings has a definite relationship to learning mathematics—or any other learning. Let us hypothesize that there are five natural tendencies in students:

1. Students in contact with life problems wish to learn.
2. Students want to grow.
3. Students seek to find out.
4. Students hope to master.
5. Students desire to create.

Therefore, the teacher must develop very personal relationships with students and create a classroom climate which allows these five natural tendencies to evolve and mature.

Math Anxiety

The importance of diagnosing in the affective domain is highlighted by attention in the literature to "math anxiety." Too often only the cognitive aspects of learning are assessed and considered when dealing with learning difficulties in mathematics. However, experience of a clinical nature has made apparent to educators that emotional aspects of learning must also be considered.

Genes or Environment?

Tobias and Weissbrod (1980) presented a comprehensive summary in the *Harvard Educational Review* of studies on sex-related differences in mathematics achievement and math anxiety. They reported a survey, done by Sells at Berkeley in 1972, that showed 57 percent of males completed four years of high school mathematics compared to only 8 percent of females. The Tobias and Weissbrod summary focused on a "link between poor mathematical skills and the cultural, educational, and occupational barriers experienced by women" (p. 63). Others writing on the socialization aspects of sex-related mathematics achievement are Fennema (1977) and Sherman (1977), who argue that external pressures rather than biological factors subtly discourage females from achieving well in mathematics.

On the other hand, Jensen (1980, p. 626), Maccoby and Jacklin (1973, p. 48), and Benbow and Stanley (1980, p. 73) report lack of confidence in the cultural sex-role socialization explanation of the verbal-spatial (quantitative) sex difference. Regardless of cause, there does appear a relationship between mathematics achievement, math anxiety, and math avoidance.

The teacher must be sensitive to math anxiety and help students to learn how to cope and reduce such anxiety. Diagnostic teaching is a good strategy to help reduce anxiety since it allows for optimum attention to providing success experiences. Bandura (1977) emphasized the importance of ensuring successful performance as a method of reducing failure (and subsequent anxiety related to fear of failure).

Reducing Math Anxiety

Students can use metacognition to reduce math anxiety. *Metacognition* means thinking about one's own thinking. It is an awareness that one is thinking about something (see also Brown & DeLoache, 1978, pp. 14–15; Claparéde, 1933; Luria, 1966, p. 34; Mead, 1934, p. 100; Meichenbaum & Asarnow, 1979, p. 29; Meichenbaum & Goodman, 1971; Piaget, 1967, p. 40; Vygotsky, 1962, p. 132). Flavell (1976) explained metacognition as follows:

Metacognition refers to one's knowledge concerning one's own cognitive processes and products or anything related to them, e.g., the learning-relevant properties of information or data. For example, I am engaging in metacognition (metamemory, metalearning, metaattention, metalanguage, or whatever) if I notice that I am having more trouble learning A than B; if it strikes me that I should double-check C before accepting it as fact; if it occurs to me that I had better scrutinize each and every alternative in any multiple-choice-type task situation before deciding which is the best one; if I sense that I had better make a note of D because I may forget it; if I think to ask someone about E to see if I have it right. . . . Metacognition refers among other things to the active monitoring and consequent regulation and orchestration of these processes in relation to the cognitive objects or data on which they bear, usually in the service of some concrete goal or objective. (p. 232)

Meichenbaum and Goodman (1971) used the following modeling and rehearsal procedures as a strategy to help children reduce undesirable behavior. The strategy may also be used to reduce math anxiety:

1. problem definition ("What is it I have to do?")
2. focusing attention plus response guidance ("Be careful . . . draw the line down.")
3. self-reinforcement ("Good, I'm doing fine.")
4. self-evaluative coping skills plus error-correcting options ("That's okay, even if I make an error I can go slowly."). (p. 228)

PART 3

SYNTHESIS OF
DIAGNOSTIC TEACHING

The success of the instructional component of the Diagnostic Teaching Cycle (DTC) is dependent upon valid identification of strengths and weaknesses in mathematics and correct hypotheses. Instructional goals and objectives must then be selected that reflect the "real" needs of the student or class. Examples of instructional objectives are listed in Chapter 8 under the heading "Analysis" and in Chapter 9 under "Diagnosed Difficulties." Computational errors may be thought of as a symptom of underlying problems. They serve as a helpful tool in observing mathematics performance. The computational errors presented in this section of the book are useful as a vehicle for clinical probes and interviewing. For example, once teachers analyze computational errors they should ask students to tell their thinking: "Tell me how you got this answer." "Tell me your thinking." "Explain why you wrote the 4 here." "Go through the steps out loud that you used to find the answer to this problem." It is from the clinical data that hypotheses may be formulated.

Cognitive monitoring, discussed in Part two, is a useful technique to help students become aware of their thought processes. Probes to self provide students with a strategy for self-diagnosis. Reflective thought can be a self-initiated tool for assessing one's own strengths and weaknesses in learning. Students should be encouraged to use their individual profiles (see Appendix D) to become aware of peaks and valleys in various test performances. The class profile (see Appendix E) should also be used with the students as another way of involving them in self-evaluation.

8

Common Errors
Children Make in
Elementary School Mathematics

The following are examples of common errors* made in elementary school mathematics. This list may serve as an aid in identifying computational errors.

Analysis	*Example*

1. Lacks mastery of basic addition facts

$$\begin{array}{r} 3 \\ +4 \\ \hline 7 \end{array} \begin{array}{|c} 2 \\ 3 \\ \hline 4 \end{array}$$

2. Lacks mastery of basic subtraction facts

$$\begin{array}{r} 3 \\ -2 \\ \hline 1 \end{array} \begin{array}{|c} 8 \\ 5 \\ \hline 2 \end{array}$$

3. Lacks mastery of basic multiplication facts

$$\begin{array}{r} 3 \quad 2 \\ \times \quad 3 \\ \hline 86 \end{array}$$

4. Lacks mastery of basic division facts.

$$35 \div 5 = 6$$

$$9 \overline{\smash{\big)}\ \begin{array}{r} 6 \\ 56 \\ -56 \\ \hline 0 \end{array}}$$

5. Does not complete addition:
   a. Does not write renamed number

$$\begin{array}{r} 85 \\ +43 \\ \hline 28 \end{array}$$

   b. Leaves out numbers in column addition

$$\begin{array}{r} 4 \\ 8 \\ 2 \longleftarrow \\ +3 \\ \hline 15 \end{array}$$

6. Does not add by bridging endings— should think $5 + 9 = 14$, so $35 + 9 = 44$

$$\begin{array}{r} 35 \\ +9 \\ \hline 33 \end{array}$$

---

*Many of the errors listed in this chapter were suggested by Richard Brice, University of North Carolina, Chapel Hill.

| *Analysis* | *Example* |

7a. Lacks additive identity concept in addition

$$\begin{array}{r} 35 \\ +\,20 \\ \hline 50 \end{array}$$

7b. Error in addition of partial product

$$\begin{array}{r} 432 \\ \times\,57 \\ \hline 3\ \cancel{0}\ 24 \\ 21\ \cancel{6}\ 0 \\ 24\ \cancel{0}\ 24 \\ \hline \end{array}$$

8. Confuses multiplicative identity within addition operation

$$\begin{array}{r} 71 \\ +\,13 \\ \hline 73 \end{array}$$

9. Lacks facility with addition algorithm:
   a. Add units to units *and* tens

$$\begin{array}{r} 37 \\ +\ \ 2 \\ \hline 59 \end{array}$$

   b. Adds tens to tens *and* hundreds

$$\begin{array}{r} 342 \\ +\ 36 \\ \hline 678 \end{array}$$

   c. Adds units to tens *and* hundreds

$$\begin{array}{r} 132 \\ +\ 6 \\ \hline 798 \end{array}$$

   d. Is unable to add horizontally:
      Thinks: $3+7+1=11$; writes 1
      $\qquad\quad 4+3=7\ (+1\ \text{carried}=8)$
      $\qquad\quad 5\ \ \ =5$

      May add zero to make sum greater than largest addend: 1850

$345+7+13=185$

$$\begin{array}{r} 8 \\ 5 \\ \hline 185 \end{array}$$

   e. Does not regroup; treats each column as separate addition example

$$\begin{array}{r} 23 \\ +\ 8 \\ \hline 211 \end{array}$$

10. Does not complete subtraction

$$\begin{array}{r} 582 \\ -\ 35 \\ \hline 47 \end{array}$$

Analysis	*Example*

11. Lacks additive identity concept in subtraction

$$\begin{array}{r} 43 \\ -20 \\ \hline 20 \end{array}$$

12. Confuses role of zero in subtraction with role of zero in multiplication

$$\begin{array}{r} 37 \\ -20 \\ \hline 10 \end{array}$$

13. Lacks facility with subtraction algorithm
    a. Subtracts top digit from bottom digit whenever regrouping is involved with zero in minuend

$$\begin{array}{r} 30 \\ -18 \\ \hline 28 \end{array}$$

    b. Subtracts smaller digit from larger at all times to avoid renaming

$$\begin{array}{r} 273 \\ -639 \\ \hline 446 \end{array}$$

14. When there are fewer digits in subtrahend:
    a. Subtracts units from units *and* from tens (*and* hundreds)

$$\begin{array}{r} 783 \\ -2 \\ \hline 561 \end{array}$$

    b. Subtracts tens from tens *and* hundreds

$$\begin{array}{r} 783 \\ -\;23 \\ \hline 560 \end{array}$$

15. Confuses role of zero in multiplication with multiplicative identity

$7 \times 0 = 7$

16. Rewrites a numeral without computing

$$\begin{array}{r} 72 \\ +15 \\ \hline 77 \end{array}$$

$$\begin{array}{r} 32 \\ \times\;3 \\ \hline 36 \end{array}$$

17. Does not regroup units to tens

$$\begin{array}{r} 37 \\ +\;25 \\ \hline 52 \end{array}$$

Analysis	*Example*

18. Does not regroup tens to hundreds (or hundreds to thousands)

$$\begin{array}{r} 973 \\ +862 \\ \hline 735 \end{array}$$

19. Regroups when unnecessary

$$\begin{array}{r} 43 \\ +\ 24 \\ \hline 77 \end{array}$$

20. Writes regrouped tens digit in units place, carries units digit (writes the 1 and carries the 2 from "12")

$$\begin{array}{r} ② \\ 35 \\ +\ 7 \\ \hline 51 \end{array}$$

21. Does not rename tens digit after regrouping

$$\begin{array}{r} 54 \\ -\ 9 \\ \hline 55 \end{array}$$

22. Does not rename hundreds digit after regrouping

$$\begin{array}{r} 532 \\ -181 \\ \hline 451 \end{array}$$

23. Does not rename hundreds or tens when renaming units

$$\begin{array}{r} 906 \\ -238 \\ \hline 778 \end{array}$$

24. Does not rename tens when zero is in tens place, although hundreds are renamed

$$\begin{array}{r} 803 \\ -478 \\ \hline 335 \end{array}$$

25. When there are two zeroes in minuend, renames hundreds twice but does not rename tens

$$\begin{array}{r} 5 \\ \cancel{6}.. \\ \cancel{7}00 \\ -326 \\ \hline 284 \end{array}$$

26. Decreases hundreds digit by one when unnecessary

$$\begin{array}{r} 3\ 7\ 1 \\ -1\ 3\ 4 \\ \hline 1\ 3\ 7 \end{array}$$

Analysis	*Example*

27. Uses units place factor as addend

$$\begin{array}{r} 32 \\ \times\ \ 4 \\ \hline 126 \end{array}$$

28. Adds regrouped number to tens but does not multiply

     * $7 \times\ 5 = 35$;
       $30 + 30 = 60$

$$\begin{array}{r} 35 \\ \times\ \ 7 \\ \hline 65* \end{array}$$

29. Multiplies digits within one factor

     * $4 \times\ \ 1 =\ \ 4$;
       $1 \times 30 = 30$

$$\begin{array}{r} 31 \\ \times\ \ 4 \\ \hline 34* \end{array}$$

30. Multiplies by only one number

$$\begin{array}{r} 457 \\ \times\ \ 12 \\ \hline 914 \end{array}$$

31. "Carries" wrong number

$$\begin{array}{r} 8 \\ 67 \\ \times\ \ 40 \\ \hline 3220 \end{array}$$

32. Does not multiply units times tens

$$\begin{array}{r} 32 \\ \times\ \ 24 \\ \hline 648 \end{array}$$

33. Does not add regrouped number

$$\begin{array}{r} 37 \\ \times\ \ 7 \\ \hline 219 \end{array}$$

34. Reverses divisor with dividend

   *Thinks $6 \div 3$ instead of $30 \div 6$

$$6\overline{)\ 30}^{\ \ 2*}$$

35. Fails to complete division; stops at first partial quotient

$$\begin{array}{r} 50\ \ \\ 7\overline{)\ 370} \\ \underline{350} \end{array}$$

Analysis	*Example*

36. Does not complete division because of incompleted subtraction

$$
\begin{array}{r}
1)\ 41 \\
40) \\
7\overline{)\ 3\ 9\ 7} \\
-2\ 8\ 0 \\
\overline{7} \\
\overline{7}
\end{array}
$$

37. Fails to complete division; leaves remainder equal to or greater than divisor

$$
\begin{array}{r}
80\ \text{rem}\ 9 \\
9\overline{)\ 729} \\
720 \\
\overline{9}
\end{array}
$$

38. Subtracts incorrectly within the division algorithm

$$
\begin{array}{r}
3)\ 73\ \text{rem}\ 1 \\
70) \\
3\overline{)\ 230} \\
-21 \\
\overline{10} \longleftarrow \\
-9 \\
\overline{1}
\end{array}
$$

39. Ignores remainder because:
    a. Does not complete subtraction
    b. Does not *see* need for further computation
    c. Does not know what to do with "2" if subtraction occurs; so does not compute further

$$
\begin{array}{r}
80 \\
7\overline{)\ 562} \\
560
\end{array}
$$

40. Confuses place value of quotient by adding extra zero

$$
\begin{array}{r}
20 \\
30\overline{)\ 60}
\end{array}
$$

41. Omits zero in quotient

$$
\begin{array}{r}
30\ \text{rem}\ 3 \\
4\overline{)\ 1203} \\
1200 \\
\overline{3}
\end{array}
$$

Analysis	*Example*

42. Does not complete multiplication within division algorithm

$$\begin{array}{r} 1)\ 201 \text{ rem } 3 \\ 200) \\ 3\overline{)\ 603} \\ \underline{600} \\ 3 \end{array}$$

43. Confuses place value in division:
   a. Considers thousands divided by units as hundreds divided by units

$$\begin{array}{r} 1) \\ 200)\ 201 \\ 3\overline{)\ 6003} \\ \underline{6000} \\ 3 \\ \underline{3} \end{array}$$

   b. Records partial quotient as tens instead of units

$$\begin{array}{r} 50) \\ 100)\ 150 \\ 7\overline{)\ 735} \\ -700 \\ \overline{35} \\ \underline{35} \end{array}$$

   c. Omits zero needed to show no units in quotient

$$\begin{array}{r} 2 \text{ rem } 1 \\ 3\overline{)\ 61} \\ \underline{6} \\ 1 \end{array}$$

9

Instruction for Common Difficulties in Mathematics

Diagnosed Difficulties	*Suggestions and Reisman Resources*
Incorrect writing of digits—0 to 9.	Make use of all of the child's senses during instruction. Use cutout digits for the student to trace with his or her fingers. Use felt, sandpaper, clay for digits. Have student form digits in sand.
Does not understand place value	A distinction should be made between counting one-by-one and moving from 9 to 10, and exchanging 10 units for one ten. Furthermore, multiplication is involved in generating place value as well as in finding the value of a digit in a numeral by multiplying face times place value. However, place value is typically taught in first grade while multiplication is not introduced until late second or third grade. (See Reisman & Kauffman, 1980, pp. 152–159 and Reisman, 1981, chapter 3, for instructional procedures on place value.)
Errors when adding with renaming	a. Review place value. Start at the concrete level by having child combine 5 tongue depressors with 9. Group 10 of the 14 as 1 ten and there will be 4 ones extra. See Reisman (1981) on use of counting boards as an instructional procedure. b. Have child record as follows:

$$
\begin{array}{c|c}
\text{tens} & \text{ones} \\
\hline
 & 9 \\
+ & 5 \\
\hline
1 & 4 \\
\end{array}
$$

c. Next move to the symbolic level using numerals:

$$
\begin{array}{r}
25 \\
+\ 9 \\
\hline
14 \\
20 \\
\hline
34 \\
\end{array}
$$

| *Diagnosed*
Difficulties | *Suggestions and Reisman Resources* |

Diagnosed
Difficulties

Suggestions and Reisman Resources

Then introduce the standard algorithm:

```
  25
+  9
————
  34
```

Errors in subtracting
with renaming

    a. Review addition with renaming as shown pre-
viously. Use the same example but now subtract
(25 − 9). Show two groups of 10 and 5 units.

TENS   UNITS

//////////   /////

//////////

    b. Have child record this in place value chart:

Tens   *Ones*

2   5

    c. Next attempt to take 9 tongue depressors away.
But, there are not enough to do this. Thus, take
the rubber band off one bundle of 10 and count
them all out as 15 units. Place these in the units
position, and then you can remove 9 tongue depressors.

    d. Next record problem in a place-value chart as
shown and compute.

tens	units
2	5
−	9
1	15
−	9
1	6

Diagnosed Difficulties	*Suggestions and Reisman Resources*
Does not appear to understand additive identity, e.g., $n+0=n$	a. Combine a set (A) with the null (empty) set to show that the number property of these two sets is the same as for the first set (A). See also Reisman (1981, pp. 79–85). b. Provide practice as in the following: $4+0=4$, $9+0=9$, $73+0=73$, etc.

Does not appear to understand multiplicative identity, e.g., $n \times 1 = n$

a. Use picture to show: 1×5 and 3×1

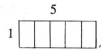

3 × 1

b. Next use equations.

$$3 \times \square = 3$$
$$3 \times 1 = \square$$
$$3 \times 1 =$$
$$\square \times 1 = 3$$

Errors when multiplying with renaming: e.g., 2×36

a. Review the distributive property of multiplication over addition.

$$2 \times 36 = 2 \times (30 + 6)$$
$$= (2 \times 30) +$$
$$(2 \times 6)$$
$$= 60 + 12$$
$$= 72$$

Then compare this algorithm with vertical algorithm:

$$
\begin{array}{rrr}
36 = & 30 & 6 \\
\times 2 & \times 2 & \times 2 \\
\hline
12 & 60 & +12 \\
60 & & \\
\hline
72 = & & 72
\end{array}
$$

See also Reisman (1981, Chapter 7).

b. Use diagrams

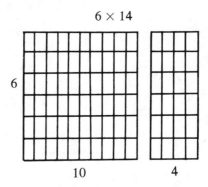

6×14

6

10   4

$$6 \times 14 = 6 \times (10 + 4)$$
$$= (6 \times 10) + (6 \times 4)$$
$$= 60 + 24$$
$$= 84$$

Cannot rename
equivalent frac-
tions

a. Concrete level:
Compare equivalent regions using cutouts.

Model Whole

$\dfrac{1}{2}$	

Cut second whole into halves

$\dfrac{1}{4}$			

Cut third whole into fourths

$\dfrac{1}{8}$							

Cut fourth whole into eighths

Place four eighths over ½ and two fourths over ½.

Diagnosed
Difficulties

Suggestions and Reisman Resources

b. Diagrams:
Compare equivalent regions.

$$1/2 = 2/4 = 4/8$$

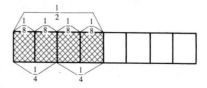

c. Symbolic level: Use multiplicative identity.

$$1/2 \times 1 = \square/4$$
$$1/2 \times 2/2 = 2/4$$

The equation $2 \times \square = 4$ gives you cue for special name for 1; in this case 2/2.

Makes errors when adding fractions with same denominators: e.g., $1/3 + 1/3 =$

a. Use concrete level. Combine ¼ and ¼ pieces of whole and count to obtain two fourths (2/4).

b. Use this algorithm:

$$1/4 + 1/4 = \frac{1 + 1}{4} = 2/4$$

Makes errors when adding fractions with different denominators: e.g., $1/4 + 1/2 =$

Prerequisite is multiplying fraction by fraction:

$$1/2 \times 2/2 = 2/4$$

a. Concrete level:
Use fractional pieces.

$$1/4 = 1/4$$

1/4	

$$1/2 = 2/4$$

1/4	1/4	

Diagnosed Difficulties	*Suggestions and Reisman Resources*

b. Symbolic level:

$$1/4 = 1/4$$
$$* + 1/2 = 2/4$$
$$\overline{ 3/4}$$

*Renaming 1/2 as 2/4

$$\frac{1}{2} \times \frac{2}{\boxed{2}} = \frac{2}{4}$$

Child must think 2 times what number yields 4? This gives a special name for 1 in the form $\frac{2}{2}$.

Then find the equivalent of $\frac{1}{2}$ in fourths by multiplying the fractions $\frac{1}{2}$ by $\frac{2}{2}$.

Makes errors when adding decimal fractions

Write numerals in vertical position

$$5.06$$
$$.789$$
$$\underline{+19.1}$$

by placing decimal dots under each other. Either fill in empty spaces with zeros or round to the least precise addend. Then, add as with whole numbers. Use of graph paper helps align digits.

Makes errors when multiplying decimal fractions, e.g., $.5 \times .03 =$

a. Rename $.5 \times .03$ to $(5 \times 3) \times (.1 \times .01)$. Use associative properties.
Multiply whole numbers: $5 \times 3 = 15$. Multiply place values: tenths $\times$ hundredths = thousandths. Decide on number of decimal places thousandths take up: *tenths hundredths thousandths*
Show number of places needed in this way:

.___ ___ ___

Diagnosed Difficulties

Suggestions and Reisman Resources

Then write in face value (15) so that the last place is filled:

.____ 1____ 5____ .

Fill in empty places with zeros:

.__0__ __1__ __5__.

b. Notice that the number of decimal places in the product is the same as the number of decimal places in factors, e.g.,

$$.5 \times .0\ 3 = .0\ 1\ 5$$

Makes errors when dividing a decimal fraction by a decimal fraction, e.g., $.25 \div .5 = \square$

a. Write the division as a fraction.

.25/.5

b. Multiply the denominator by the multiple of ten that will yield a whole number:

$$\frac{.25}{.5} \times \frac{10}{10} = \frac{2.50}{5.0} = \frac{2.5}{5}$$

c. Divide the face values:

$$25 \div 5 = 5$$

d. Insert the same number of decimal places in the quotient as are now in the dividend:

$$.25 \div .5 = \square$$

(multiply by 10)

$$2.5 \div 5 = .5$$

Appendix A

Selected Answers to SAMI

Part 1: Grades K–2

7c. $3 = 3$ $12 = 12$

8c. $6 < 9, 3 < 5, 4 > 2, 8 < 9$

9a.

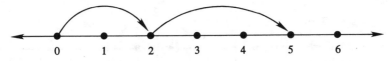

9b. 6

9c. $2 + 3 = 3 + 2, \square + \blacksquare = \blacksquare + \square$

9d. $(2 + 3) + 4 = 2 + (3 + 4), (8 + 6) + 7 = 8 + (6 + 7)$

9e. $3 + 0 = 3$

10a. $2 + 2 + 2 = 6, 3 \times 2 = 6$

10b. $4 \times 3 = 12$

10c. 100

11b. 100

11f.

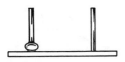

12a.   47
        − 32
        ─────
         15

12b. $6 - 4 = 2$

Part 2: Grades 3–4

12c. $4 + 7 = 11$ $11 - 7 = 4$ $11 - 4 = 7$
12d. $5 - 3 = 2$
12e. 14, *11*, 10
      10, 7, *6*
      9, *15*, 12, 11

12h.   62   35
        − 48   − 19
        ─────   ─────
         14   16

9h.   37   59
        + 26   + 74
        ─────   ─────
         63   133

9i.   13
        + 9
        ─────
         22

10d. $3 \times 5 = 15$
10e.

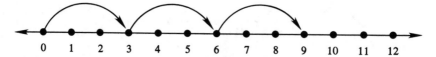

10f. $18 = 3 \times 6$ $18 = 2 \times 9$ $18 = 2 \times 3 \times 3$
10g. $5(3 + 6) = 5(3) + 5(6)$, $\square(* + @) = \square* + \square@$
13a.

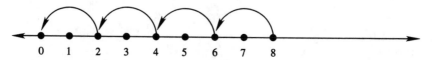

13c. $18 \div 3 = 6$ $6 \times 3 = 18$
14a. 2,3,5,7,11,13,17,19,23
14b. 2,11
14c. $24 = 2 \times 2 \times 2 \times 3$

10h. LCM = 24
10i. GCF = 12
15a.

 or 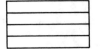 or

15c. 5/6
15d. 2/5
15e. 2/2, 3/3, 4/4, . . .
15f.

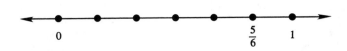

15g.

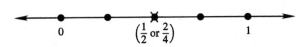

15h. 1/2 = 2/4 = 3/6 = 4/8, . . .
15i. 8/15, 35/48

Part 3: Grades 5–6

10j. 20, 28,12
    40,56,24
    30,42,18

15j. $15\frac{3}{4},$ $3\frac{1}{2} \times 2\frac{1}{4} = \left(3 + \frac{1}{2}\right) \times \left(2 + \frac{1}{4}\right)$

$$= (3 \times 2) + \left(3 \times \frac{1}{4}\right) + \left(\frac{1}{2} \times 2\right) + \left(\frac{1}{2} \times \frac{1}{4}\right)$$

$$= 6 \quad + \frac{3}{4} + \frac{2}{2} + \frac{1}{8}$$

$$= \quad 7 + \frac{3}{4} + \frac{1}{8}$$

$$= \quad 7 + \frac{6}{8} + \frac{1}{8}$$

$$= 7 \quad + \frac{7}{8}$$

$$= 7 \quad \frac{7}{8}$$

15k. $\dfrac{7}{12} \div \dfrac{3}{4} = \dfrac{7}{\cancel{12}} \times \dfrac{\cancel{4}\,^1}{3} = \dfrac{7}{9}$

$\quad\quad\quad\quad\quad\quad\quad^3$

$\quad\dfrac{35}{27} \div \dfrac{7}{3} = \dfrac{5}{9}$

15l. $\dfrac{5}{4}, \dfrac{7}{8} + \dfrac{2}{3} = \dfrac{21}{24} + \dfrac{16}{24} = \dfrac{37}{24} = 1\dfrac{13}{24}$

15m. 2/3, 5/8

16a. .2, .07

16b. 4.79, 5.03, 4.39

16c. .046, .0516, 17.52

16d. .6, .3, 69

16e. .5, .75, .5, $.\overline{6}$ or $.\overline{66}$

16f. 23/100, 25/100 or 1/4, 3/10

16g. .75

16h. 5.1

17a. 130°

17b.

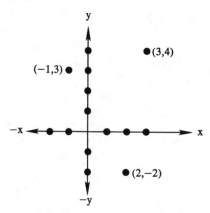

17c. 60mm, 3000m

17d. 36 cm²

Part 4: Grades 7–8

17e. 24 cm^2

17f. d = 4 cm

17g. C = πd   d = 2r
        = π 12 cm or 12πcm

17h. A = 1/2bh
        = 1/2 (12)
        = 6 cm^2

17i.

17j.

17k.

18a. 1/2 or $\frac{5}{10}$

18b. bears—5, tigers—4

18c. Ann's mean equals 79; Barbara's mean = 73.7; Catherine's mean = 79.6; Catherine has the highest mean score.

Appendix B

Table of Specification for SAMI

SAMI Part 1: Grades K–2

Behavior

Content	Show	Write	Interpret	Compute
Proximity	1a, 1b			
Spatial Relations	2a–2f			
Size	3a, 3b			
Numeration	4b, 7c	4a, 4c	7a	
Cardinality	5a, 5b			
Classification	6b		6a	
Equivalent sets	7b			
Nonequivalence	8a, 8b	8c		
Addition of whole numbers	9c, 9d, 9e	9a, 9b		9f, 9g
Multiplication of whole numbers	10a	10b	10c	
Place Value	11a, 11b, 11f		11c, 11d, 11e	11g
Subtraction of whole numbers			12b	12a

SAMI Part 2: Grades 3—4

Behavior

Content	Show	Write	Interpret	Compute
Subtraction of whole numbers	12f	12d	12c, 12g	12e, 12h
Addition of whole numbers	9h		9i	
Multiplication of whole numbers	10g	10f, 10h, 10i	10d, 10e	
Division of whole numbers	13a, 13b	13d	13c	13e
Prime Numbers	15a, 15f	14a, 14c	14b	
Fractions		15e, 15d, 15g, 15h	15b, 15c	15i

SAMI Part 3: Grades 5—6

Behavior

Content	Show	Interpret	Translate	Compute
Multiplication of whole numbers				10j
Fractions				15j–15m
Decimals		16g	16e, 16f	16a–16d, 16h
Geometry	17b			17a, 17c, 17d

SAMI Part 4: Grades 7—8

Behavior

Content	Show	Identify	Interpret	Compute
Geometry	17i, 17j	17k		17e–17h
Probability and Statistics			18b, 18c	18a

Appendix C

Psychological Nature of Items Comprising the SAMI and Mode of Representation

Item	Psychological Nature	Mode	Item	Psychological Nature	Mode
Part 1					
4a	relationship	symbol	10c	generalization	symbol
4c	arbitrary association	symbol	11a	concept	iconic
7a	concept	symbol	11b	generalization	iconic-symbol
7b	concept	iconic	11f	generalization	iconic
7c	relationship	symbol	11g	generalization	symbol
8a	concept	iconic	12a	generalization	symbol
8b	relationship	iconic	12b	generalization	iconic-symbol
8c	relationship	symbol			
9a	generalization	iconic			
9b	generalization	iconic	*Part 2*		
9c	generalization	symbol	12c	generalization	symbol
9d	generalization	symbol	12d	generalization	symbol
9e	generalization	symbol	12e	generalization	symbol
9g	generalization	symbol	12h	generalization	symbol
10a	generalization	iconic-symbol	9h	generalization	symbol
			9i	generalization	symbol
10b	generalization	iconic-symbol	10d	generalization	iconic
			10e	generalization	iconic

Item	Psychological Nature	Mode	Item	Psychological Nature	Mode
Part 2—Cont.					
10f	generalization	symbol	15l	generalization	symbol
10g	generalization	symbol	15m	generalization	symbol
10h	generalization	symbol	16a	generalization	symbol
10i	generalization	symbol	16b	generalization	symbol
13a	generalization	iconic	16c	generalization	symbol
13b	generalization	iconic	16d	generalization	symbol
13c	generalization	symbol	16e	generalization	symbol
13d	generalization	iconic	16f	relationship	symbol
13e	generalization	symbol	16g	generalization	symbol
14a	concept	symbol	16h	generalization	symbol
14b	concept	symbol	17a	generalization	iconic
14c	generalization	symbol	17b	generalization	iconic
15a	generalization	iconic	17c	relationship	symbol
15b	concept	iconic	17d	generalization	iconic
15c	generalization	iconic			
15d	generalization	iconic	*Part 4*		
15e	generalization	symbol	17e	generalization	iconic
15f	concept	iconic	17f	generalization	iconic
15g	relationship	iconic	17g	generalization	symbol
15h	relationship	symbol	17h	generalization	iconic
15i	generalization	symbol	17i	concept	iconic
			17j	relationship	iconic
Part 3			17k	concept	iconic
10j	generalization	symbol	18a	generalization	symbol
15j	generalization	symbol	18b	generalization	iconic
15k	generalization	symbol	18c	generalization	symbol

Appendix D

Individual SAMI Profile

Part 1: Grades K–2

Name _____ Grade in School _____

CA _____ MA _____ Date _____

Step 1: Circle incorrect items.

A. Proximity, Spatial Relations, Size

1a,1b,2a,2b,2c,2d,2e,2f,3a,3b,

B. Numeration

4a,4b,4c,7a,7c

C. Cardinality, Classification, Equivalence, Nonequivalence

5a,5b,6a,6b,7b,8a,8b,8c

D. Operations on Whole Numbers

9a,9b,9c,9d,9e,9f,9g,10a,10b,10c, 11a,11b,11c,11d,11e,11f,11g,12a, 12b

Step 2: Count the number of correct items (not circled) for each group.

Step 3: To find percent of items correct within each group, first circle number of items correct in each box below, and then circle equivalent percent correct.

A.

No. of Items Correct	Equi. % Correct
10	100
9	90
8	80
7	70
6	60
5	50
4	40
3	30
2	20
1	10

B.

# Correct	% Correct
5	100
4	80
3	60
2	40
1	20

C.

# Correct	% Correct
8	100
7	88
6	75
5	63
4	50
3	38
2	25
1	13

D.

No. of Items Correct	Approx. % Correct	# Correct	Approx. % Correct
19	100	9	48
18	95	8	42
17	90	7	37
16	85	6	32
15	80	5	27
14	75	4	21
13	69	3	16
12	64	2	11
11	58	1	5
10	53		

Step 4: On Chart below, graph percentage correct in each group to show the child's strengths and weaknesses.

Percent of Items Correct

100
80
60
40
20
0

A. Proximity, Spatial Relations, Size	B. Numeration	C. Cardinality, Classification, Equivalence, Nonequivalence	D. Operations on Whole Numbers

Individual SAMI Profile

Part 2: Grades 3—4

Step 1: Circle incorrect items.

A. Cardinality, Classification, Equivalence, Nonequivalence

6a, 6b, 7b, 8a, 8b, 8c

B. Operations on Whole Numbers

9a, 9b, 9c, 9d, 9e, 9f, 9g, 9h, 9i,10a,10b,10c,10d,10e,10f,10g, 10h,10i,11a,11b,11c,11d,11e,11f, 11g,12a,12b,12c,12d,12e,12f,12g, 12h,13a,13b,13c,13d,13e

C. Prime Numbers

14a, 14b, 14c

D. Fractions

15a,15b,15c,15d,15e, 15f,15g,15h,15i

Step 2: Count the number of correct items (not circled) for each group.

Step 3: To find percent of items correct within each group, first circle number of items correct in each box below, and then circle equivalent percent correct.

A.

# Corr.	% Corr.
6	100
5	85
4	68
3	51
2	34
1	17

B.

# Corr.	% Corr.	# Corr.	% Corr.	# Corr.	% Corr.	# Corr.	% Corr.
38	100	30	79	20	52	10	26
37	97	29	75	19	49	9	23
36	95	28	73	18	47	8	21
35	91	27	70	17	44	7	18
34	89	26	68	16	42	6	16
33	87	25	65	15	39	5	13
32	84	24	62	14	36	4	10
31	81	23	60	13	34	3	8
		22	57	12	31	2	5
		21	55	11	29	1	3

C.

# Corr.	% Corr.
3	100
2	66
1	33

D.

# Corr.	% Corr.
9	100
8	88
7	77
6	66
5	55
4	44
3	33
2	22
1	11

Step 4: On Chart below, graph percentage correct in each group to show the child's strengths and weaknesses.

Percent of Items Correct

100
80
60
40
20
0

A. Cardinality, Classification, Equivalence, Nonequivalence   B. Operations on Whole Numbers   C. Prime Numbers   D. Fractions

Individual SAMI Profile

Part 3: Grades 5-6

Name _____ Grade in School _____

CA _____ MA _____ Date _____

Step 1: Circle incorrect items.

A. Operations on Whole Numbers	B. Prime Numbers	C. Fractions	D. Decimals	E. Geometry
9c, 9d, 9e, 9f, 9g, 9h, 9i,10a 10b,10c,10d,10e,10f,10g,10h,10i, 10j,11a,11b,11c,11d,11e,11f,11g, 12a,12b,12c,12d,12e,12f,12g,12h, 13a,13b,13c,13d,13e	14a, 14b, 14c	15a,15b,15c,15d, 15e,15f,15g,15h, 15i,15j,15k,15l, 15m	16a,16b,16c,16d, 16e,16f,16g,16h	17a,17b,17c, 17d

Step 2: Count the number of correct items (not circled) for each group.

Step 3: To find percent of items correct within each group, first circle number of items correct in each box below, and then circle equivalent percent correct.

A.

# Corr.	% Corr.	# Corr.	% Corr.	# Corr.	% Corr.	# Corr.	% Corr.
37	100	27	73	17	46	7	19
36	97	26	70	16	43	6	16
35	95	25	68	15	41	5	14
34	92	24	65	14	38	4	11
33	89	23	62	13	35	3	8
32	86	22	59	12	32	2	5
31	84	21	57	11	30	1	3
30	81	20	54	10	27		
29	78	19	51	9	24		
28	76	18	49	8	22		

B.

# Corr.	% Corr.
3	100
2	66
1	33

C.

# Corr.	% Corr.
13	100
12	92
11	85
10	77
9	69
8	62
7	54
6	46
5	38
4	31
3	23
2	15
1	8

D.

# Corr.	% Corr.
8	100
7	88
6	75
5	63
4	50
3	38
2	25
1	13

E.

# Corr.	% Corr.
4	100
3	75
2	50
1	25

Step 4: On Chart below, graph percentage correct in each group to show the child's strengths and weaknesses.

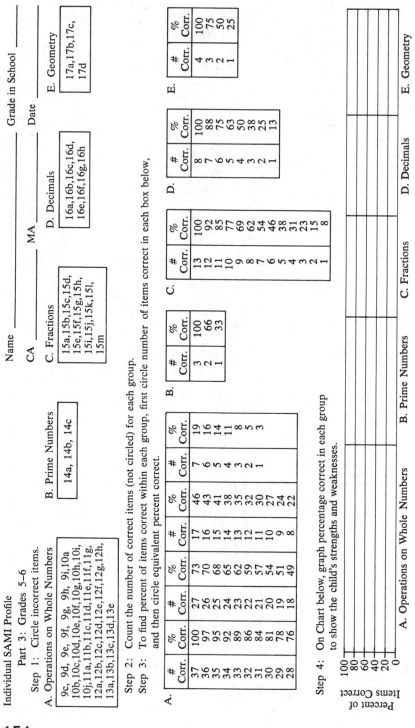

Percent of Items Correct

100
80
60
40
20
0

A. Operations on Whole Numbers | B. Prime Numbers | C. Fractions | D. Decimals | E. Geometry

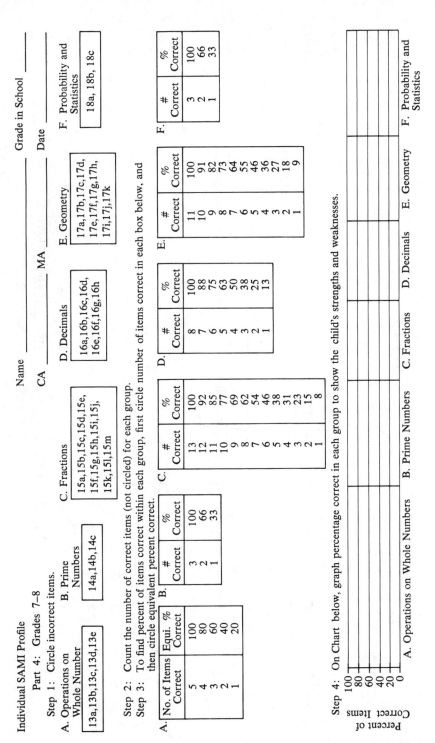

Individual SAMI Profile

Part 4: Grades 7-8

Name _____ Grade in School _____

CA _____ MA _____ Date _____

Step 1: Circle incorrect items.

A. Operations on Whole Number	B. Prime Numbers	C. Fractions	D. Decimals	E. Geometry	F. Probability and Statistics
13a,13b,13c,13d,13e	14a,14b,14c	15a,15b,15c,15d,15e, 15f,15g,15h,15i,15j, 15k,15l,15m	16a,16b,16c,16d, 16e,16f,16g,16h	17a,17b,17c,17d, 17e,17f,17g,17h, 17i,17j,17k	18a, 18b, 18c

Step 2: Count the number of correct items (not circled) for each group.

Step 3: To find percent of items correct within each group, first circle number of items correct in each box below, and then circle equivalent percent correct.

A.

No. of Items Correct	Equi. % Correct
5	100
4	80
3	60
2	40
1	20

B.

# Correct	% Correct
3	100
2	66
1	33

C.

# Correct	% Correct
13	100
12	92
11	85
10	77
9	69
8	62
7	54
6	46
5	38
4	31
3	23
2	15
1	8

D.

# Correct	% Correct
8	100
7	88
6	75
5	63
4	50
3	38
2	25
1	13

E.

# Correct	% Correct
11	100
10	91
9	82
8	73
7	64
6	55
5	46
4	36
3	27
2	18
1	9

F.

# Correct	% Correct
3	100
2	66
1	33

Step 4: On Chart below, graph percentage correct in each group to show the child's strengths and weaknesses.

Percent of Correct Items						
100						
80						
60						
40						
20						
0						
	A. Operations on Whole Numbers	B. Prime Numbers	C. Fractions	D. Decimals	E. Geometry	F. Probability and Statistics

157

Appendix E

Class SAMI Profile

Part 1: Grades K–2

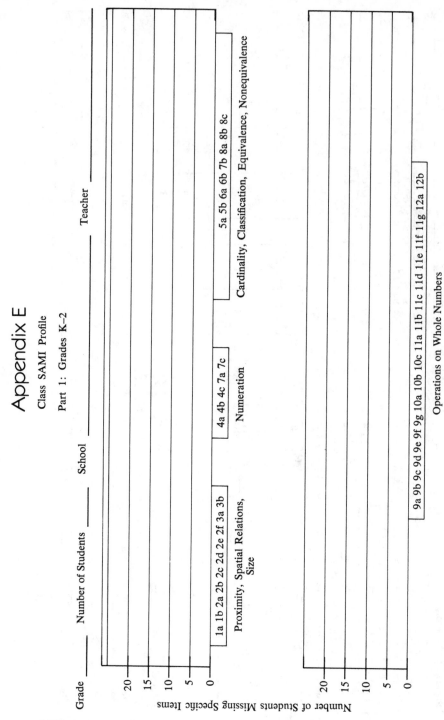

Class SAMI Profile

Part 2: Grades 3–4

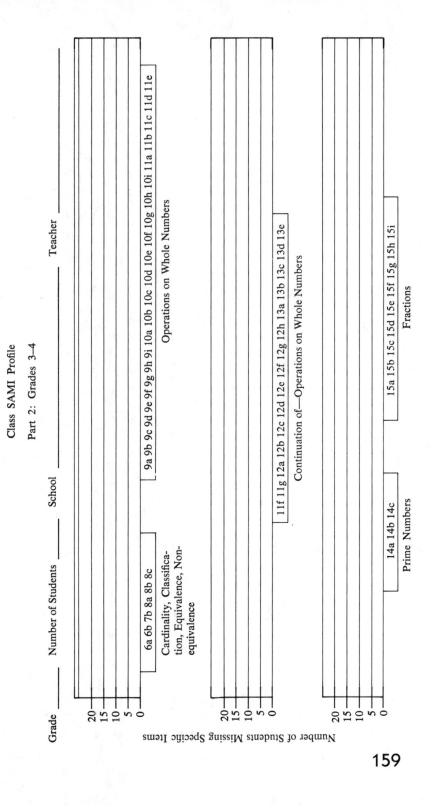

Grade _____ Number of Students _____ School _____ Teacher _____

Number of Students Missing Specific Items

6a 6b 7b 8a 8b 8c
Cardinality, Classification, Equivalence, Non-equivalence

9a 9b 9c 9d 9e 9f 9g 9h 9i 10a 10b 10c 10d 10e 10f 10g 10h 10i 11a 11b 11c 11d 11e
Operations on Whole Numbers

11f 11g 12a 12b 12c 12d 12e 12f 12g 12h 13a 13b 13c 13d 13e
Continuation of—Operations on Whole Numbers

14a 14b 14c
Prime Numbers

15a 15b 15c 15d 15e 15f 15g 15h 15i
Fractions

159

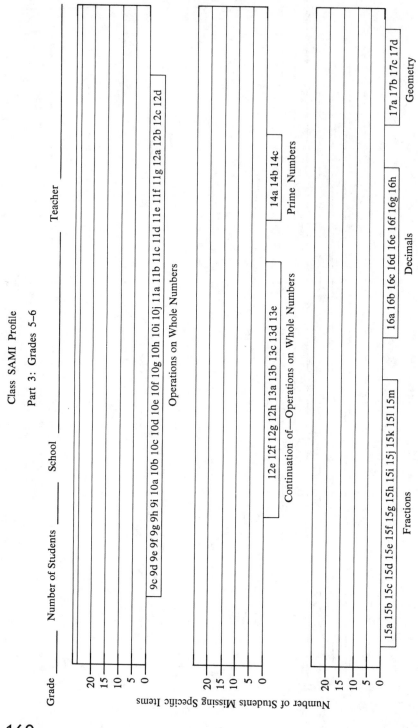

Class SAMI Profile

Part 3: Grades 5–6

Grade _____ Number of Students _____ School _____ Teacher _____

Number of Students Missing Specific Items

9c 9d 9e 9f 9g 9h 9i 10a 10b 10c 10d 10e 10f 10g 10h 10i 10j 11a 11b 11c 11d 11e 11f 11g 12a 12b 12c 12d

Operations on Whole Numbers

12e 12f 12g 12h 13a 13b 13c 13d 13e

Continuation of—Operations on Whole Numbers

14a 14b 14c

Prime Numbers

15a 15b 15c 15d 15e 15f 15g 15h 15i 15j 15k 15l 15m

Fractions

16a 16b 16c 16d 16e 16f 16g 16h

Decimals

17a 17b 17c 17d

Geometry

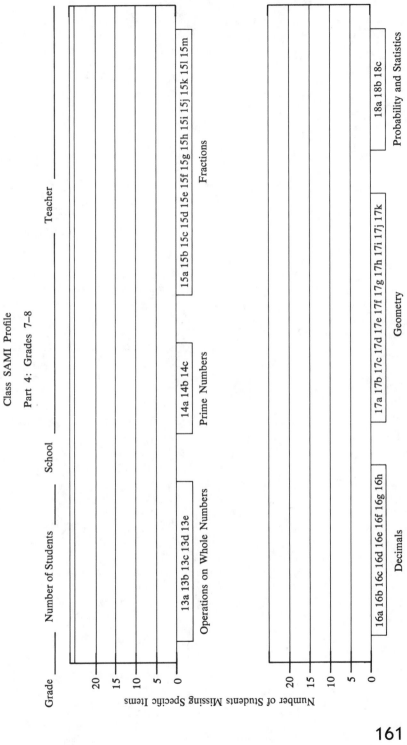

Class SAMI Profile

Part 4: Grades 7–8

Grade _____ Number of Students _____ School _____ Teacher _____

Number of Students Missing Specific Items

13a 13b 13c 13d 13e
Operations on Whole Numbers

14a 14b 14c
Prime Numbers

15a 15b 15c 15d 15e 15f 15g 15h 15i 15j 15k 15l 15m
Fractions

16a 16b 16c 16d 16e 16f 16g 16h
Decimals

17a 17b 17c 17d 17e 17f 17g 17h 17i 17j 17k
Geometry

18a 18b 18c
Probability and Statistics

161

REFERENCES

Bandura, A. B. Self-efficacy: Toward a unifying theory of behavioral change. *Psychological Review*, 1977, *84*, 191–215.

Benbow, C. P. & Stanley, J. C. Do males have a math gene? Quoted by Dennis A. Williams and Patricia King. *Newsweek,* December 15, 1980, p. 73.

Bloom, B. S.; Engelhart, M. D.; Furst, E. J.; Hill, W. H.; and Krathwohl, D. R. *Taxonomy of educational objectives, Handbook 1: Cognitive domain.* New York: David McKay Co., 1956.

Braun, C. Familiarity breeds understanding. *Arithmetic Teacher,* 1969, *16*, 316–317.

Brown, A. L., & DeLoache, J. S. Skills, plans, and self-regulation. In R. S. Siegler (Ed.), *Children's thinking: What develops?* Hillsdale, N. J.: Lawrence Erlbaum Associates, 1978.

Brownell, W. H., & Hendrickson, G. How children learn information, concepts, and generalizations. *The Forty-ninth Yearbook of the National Society for the Study of Education, Part I.* Chicago: University of Chicago Press, 1950.

Bruner, J. S. *Toward a theory of instruction.* Cambridge, Mass.: Harvard University Press, Belknap Press, 1963.

Buros, O. K. (Ed.). *The seventh mental measurements yearbook.* Highland Park, N.J.: Gryphon Press, 1972.

Carroll, J. B. A model for school learning. *Teachers College Record,* 1963, *64*, 723–733.

Claparéde, E. La genese de l'hypothese. *Archives de Psychologie,* 1933, *24*, 1–155.

Dunn, L. M., *Peabody Picture Vocabulary Test*. Circle Pines, Minn.: American Guidance Service, 1965.

Fennema, E. Influence of selected cognitive, affective, and educational variables on sex-related differences in mathematics learning and studying. *Women in Mathematics: Research Perspectives for Change*. Washington, D.C.: NIE Papers in Education and Work, November 1977. (No. 8)

Flavell, J. H. Metacognitive aspects of problem solving. In L. Resnick (Ed.), *The nature of intelligence*. Hillsdale, N. J.: Lawrence Erlbaum Associates, 1976.

Fraiberg, S. *Every child's birthright: In defense of mothering*. New York: Basic Books, 1977.

Gagne, R. M. The acquisition of knowledge. *Psychological Review*, 1962, *62*, 355–365.

Gagne, R. M. *The conditions of learning*. New York: Holt, Rinehart and Winston, 1965.

Glennon, V. J. Enrichment mathematics for the grades. In V. J. Glennon (Ed.), *Twenty-seventh Yearbook of the National Council of Teachers of Mathematics*. Washington, D.C.: National Council of Teachers of Mathematics, 1963.

Goldschmidt, M. L., & Bentler, P. M. The dimensions and measurement of conservation. *Child Development*, 1968, *39*, 787–802.(a)

Goldschmidt, M. L., & Bentler, P. M. *Concept assessment kit: Conservation*, Manual and Keys. San Diego, Calif.: Educational and Industrial Testing Service, 1968. (b)

Good, T. L., & Brophy, J. E. *Educational psychology: A realistic approach*. New York: Holt, Rinehart and Winston, 1977.

Harnischfeger, A., & Wiley, D. The teaching-learning process in elementary schools: A synoptic view. *Curriculum Inquiry*, 1976, *6*, 1–43.

Horn, A. The uneven distribution of the effects of specific factors. *Southern California Education Monographs*, No. 12. University of Southern California Press, 1941. (Later unpublished research studies, Evaluation section, Los Angeles City Schools.)

Jensen, A. R. *Bias in mental testing*. New York: The Free Press, 1980.

Kagan, J., Kearsley, R. B., & Zelazo, P. R. *Infancy: Its place in human development*. Cambridge, Mass.: Harvard University Press, 1978.

Kessler, S. J., & McKenna, W. *Gender: An ethnomethodological approach*. New York: John Wiley & Sons, 1978.

Krathwohl, D. R., Bloom, B. S., & Masia, B. B. *Taxonomy of educational objectives, Handbook 2: Affective domain*. New York: David McKay Co., 1966.

Luria, A. R. *Higher cortical functions in man*. New York: Basic Books, 1966.

Maccoby, E. E., & Jacklin, C. N. Sex differences in intellectual functioning. In *Assessment in a Pluralistic Society* (pp. 37–55). *Proceedings of the 1972 Invitational Conference on Testing Problems*. Princeton, N.J.: Educational Testing Service, 1973.

Mager, R. F. *Preparing instructional objectives*. Palo Alto, Calif.: Fearon Publishers, 1962.

Maslow, A. H. *Motivation and personality*. New York: Harper and Row, 1954.

Maslow, A. H. Some basic propositions of a growth and self-actualization psychology. In A. W. Combs (chairman) *Perceiving, Behaving, Becoming, A New Focus for Education, 1962 Yearbook* (pp. 34–39). Washington, D.C.: Association for Supervision and Curriculum Development, 1962.

McGillivray, R. H. Differences in home background between high-achieving and low-achieving gifted children: A study of 108 pupils in the city of Toronto Public Schools. *Ontario Journal of Educational Research*, 1964, *6*, 99–106.

Mead, G. H. *Mind, self, and society from the standpoint of a social behaviorist*. Chicago: University of Chicago Press, 1934.

Meichenbaum, D., & Asarnow, J. Cognitive behavior modification and metacognitive development: Implications for the classroom. In P. Kendall & S. Hollow (Eds.), *Cognitive-behavioral interventions: Theory, research, and procedures*. New York: Academic Press, 1979.

Meichenbaum, D., & Goodman, J. Training impulsive children to talk to themselves: A means of developing self-control. *Journal of Abnormal Psychology*, 1971, *77*, 115–126.

Mumpower, D. L., & Riggs, S. Overachievement in word accuracy as a result of parental pressure. *The Reading Teacher*, 1970, *23*, 741–747.

Osborn, A. F. *Applied imagination* (3rd ed.). New York: Scribners, 1963.

Osgood, C., Suci, G., & Tannenbaum, P. *The measurement of meaning*. Urbana, Ill.: University of Illinois Press, 1957.

Parnes, S. J. *Creative behavior guidebook*. New York: Scribners, 1967.

Piaget, J. *Six psychological studies*. New York: Random House, 1967.

Piaget, J. *Child's conception of number*. New York: W.W. Norton and Co., 1965.

Piaget, J. The development of time concepts in the child. In P. Hoch & J. Cuben (Eds.), *Psychopathology of Childhood* (pp. 34–44). *Proceedings of the Forty-fourth Annual Meeting of the American Psychopathological Association, June 1955*. New York: Grune and Stratton, 1955.

Piaget, J. Time perception in children. In J. T. Fraser (Ed.), *The voices of time*. New York: George Braziller, 1966.

Pierce, J. V. Personality and achievement among able high school boys. *Journal of Individual Psychology*, 1961, *17*, 101–102.

Pinard, A., & Laurendeau, M. A scale of mental development based on the theory of Piaget. *Journal of Research Science in Teaching*, 1964, *2*, 253–260.

Popham, J. W., & Baker, E. L. *Establishing instructional goals*. Englewood Cliffs, N.J.: Prentice-Hall, 1970.

Reisman, F. K. An evaluative study of cognitive acceleration in mathematics in the early school years. (Doctoral dissertation, Syracuse University, 1968). *Dissertation Abstracts*, 1969, *29*, (12). (University Microfilms No. 69–8648, 302.)

Reisman, F. K. Children's errors in telling time and a recommended teaching sequence. *The Arithmetic Teacher,* 1971, *18,* 152–55.

Reisman, F. K. *Diagnostic teaching of elementary school mathematics: Methods and content.* Skokie, Ill.: Rand McNally, 1977.

Reisman, F. K. *Teaching mathematics: Methods and content.* (2nd ed.). Boston: Houghton Mifflin, 1981.

Reisman, F. K. *Sequential Assessment in Mathematics Inventory* (Classroom Diagnosing and Concrete Kit). Columbus, Ohio: Charles E. Merrill, in press.

Reisman, F. K., Ellett, C., & Payne, D. *Sequential Assessment in Mathematics Inventory* (Technical Manual and Short Screening). Columbus, Ohio: Charles E. Merrill, in press.

Reisman, F. K., & Kauffman, S. H. *Teaching mathematics to children with special needs.* Columbus, Ohio: Charles E. Merrill, 1980.

Riley, J. F. *Creative problem solving and cognitive monitoring as instructional variables for teacher training in classroom problem solving.* Unpublished doctoral dissertation, University of Georgia, 1980.

Rogers, C. R. Significant learning: In therapy and in education. *Educational Leadership,* 1959, *16,* 4. (a)

Rogers, C. R. A theory of therapy, personality, and interpersonal relationships. In S. Koch (Ed.), *Psychology: A study of science* (Vol. 3). New York: McGraw-Hill, 1959. (b)

Rouman, J. School children's problems as related to parental factors. *Journal of Educational Research,* 1956, *50,* 105.

Sherman, J. Effects of biological factors on sex-related differences in mathematics achievement. *Women and Mathematics: Research Perspectives for Change.* Washington, D.C.: NIE Papers in Education and Work, November 1977. (No. 8)

Shotick, A. L., & Reisman, F. K. The supervisor as a creative problem solver, Module 4. *An instructional model for training LEA supervisors to assist in training teachers in best practices and exemplary models for educating handicapped students in the least restrictive environment.* Federally funded project, Southeast Learning Resource Center, HEW, BEH, Contract No. OEC–78–0017, Northeast CESA, Winterville, Georgia, 1979.

Slosson, R. L. *The Slosson Intelligence Test for Children and Adults.* East Aurora, N.Y.: Slosson Educational Publications, 1963.

Taba, H., & Elkins, D. *Teaching strategies for the culturally disadvantaged.* Chicago: Rand McNally, 1966.

Terman, L. M., & Merrill, M. A. *Stanford-Binet Intelligence Scale Manual for the Third Revision, Form L—M.* Boston: Houghton Mifflin, 1962.

Tobias, S., & Weissbrod, C. Anxiety and mathematics: An update. *Harvard Educational Review,* 1980, *50,* 63–70.

Torrance, E. P. *The search for satori and creativity.* Buffalo, N.Y.: Creative Education Foundation, 1979.

Vygotsky, L. S. *Thought and language*. Cambridge, Mass.: M.I.T. Press, 1962.

Wechsler, D. *Wechsler Intelligence Scale for Children–Revised (WISC–R)*. New York: Psychological Corporation, 1974.

Wilson, J. W. *The role of structure in verbal problem-solving in arithmetic*. Unpublished doctoral dissertation, Syracuse University, 1964.

AUTHOR INDEX

169

SUBJECT INDEX